MODERN
NATIONS
—OF THE—
WORLD

YEMEN

TITLES IN THE MODERN NATIONS OF THE WORLD SERIES INCLUDE:

Afghanistan	Japan
Argentina	Jordan
Australia	Kenya
Austria	Lebanon
Brazil	Mexico
Cambodia	Nigeria
Canada	Norway
China	Pakistan
Congo	Peru
Cuba	Philippines
Czech Republic	Poland
Egypt	Russia
England	Saudi Arabia
Ethiopia	Scotland
Finland	Somalia
France	South Africa
Germany	South Korea
Greece	Spain
Haiti	Sudan
Hungary	Sweden
India	Switzerland
Iran	Taiwan
Iraq	Thailand
Ireland	Turkey
Israel	United States
Italy	Vietnam

YEMEN

BY CHRIS EBOCH

LUCENT
BOOKS®

THOMSON

GALE

San Diego • Detroit • New York • San Francisco • Cleveland
New Haven, Conn. • Waterville, Maine • London • Munich

© 2004 by Lucent Books. Lucent Books is an imprint of The Gale Group, Inc.,
a division of Thomson Learning, Inc.

Lucent Books® and Thomson Learning™ are trademarks used herein under license.

For more information, contact
Lucent Books
27500 Drake Rd.
Farmington Hills, MI 48331-3535
Or you can visit our Internet site at http://www.gale.com

LIBRARY OF CONGRESS CATALOGING-IN-PUBLICATION DATA

Eboch, Chris
    Yemen / by Chris Eboch.
    v. cm. — (Modern nations of the world)
    Includes bibliographical references and index.
    Contents: The green land of Arabia—Occupations and independence—North and South
    fight and unite—Daily life in Yemen—The arts of Yemen—Today's challenges.
      ISBN 1-59018-240-5
      1. Yemen—Juvenile Literature. [1. Yemen.] I. Title. II. Series.
      DS247.Y48E26 2004
      953.6—dc21

                                                                        20020156250

Printed in the United States of America

CONTENTS

INTRODUCTION

AT THE CENTER OF THE WORLD

Throughout much of Yemen's history, the country has had an importance on the world stage much greater than its size or power would suggest. In ancient times, Yemen's location on the southern edge of the Arabian Peninsula put it in the middle of a major trade route that crossed continents. Traders from Europe, Asia, and Africa stopped in Yemen on their journeys, whether by land or by sea, and the country grew rich because of this.

Eventually the ancient trade routes fell into disuse, but Yemen and the region as a whole never lost their allure to the outside world. Trade between the Mediterranean and the Far East still passed through the Red Sea, and Yemen sits at the southern entrance to the Red Sea. This location attracted invaders who wanted to control that trade route. Some succeeded in subduing the local tribes that had ruled the region for centuries, and by the beginning of the twentieth century, two foreign powers ruled Yemen. The Ottoman Turks held northern Yemen, while Britain controlled southern Yemen.

The Yemeni people eventually managed to expel the foreigners, but even then their country remained divided. Over the next few decades, what had become the separate nations of North and South Yemen experimented with different forms of government, and, in the process, grew more estranged. The two nations even fought each other over territory that both claimed.

The political division in the southern Arabian Peninsula finally ended when North and South Yemen united in 1990. Today the country's elected officials are trying to make Yemen a peaceful, modern country with education available for all citizens and jobs for all who want to work. Yemen's leaders have a huge task set out for them. Many of Yemen's 18 million residents suffer from poverty, unemployment, and illiteracy. At the same time, the government is struggling to bring true unity to people who hold widely divergent political beliefs and religious ideals, and whose tribal loyalties often take precedence over national allegiance.

Today Yemen is neither rich nor powerful, yet the country still has worldwide importance. As the United States and European nations focus on the Middle East in their fight against terrorism, Yemen has again caught the attention of outsiders. Although Yemen's government denounces terrorism, some Yemeni citizens have been involved in major terrorist attacks, and Yemen itself has been the site of significant terrorist incidents. The United States is working with Yemen to control terrorism, though the partnership is an awkward one, built partly on threats and partly on financial incentives in the form of aid. If Yemen fails to stop terrorism, the possibility

Two Yemeni villagers stroll along a road. Life in Yemen remains difficult despite government efforts to improve conditions.

looms of foreign military action that could destroy Yemen's fragile progress toward prosperity. However, if Yemen pleases the United States and the European nations, these rich countries could help assure continued progress through direct aid, investment, and trade.

Foreign countries are also interested in developing Yemen's recently discovered oil reserves. So far, Yemen has relatively little oil compared with other Middle Eastern countries. But if enough oil is found, this valuable resource could finance Yemen's development as a modern country.

A FUTURE IN BALANCE

Modernization is under way, although it can create a strange blend of cultures. Travel writer Eric Hansen noted, "The jux-

taposition of past and present is one of the most striking features of Yemeni society. In Sana'a [the capital of Yemen] I had seen men in hand-forged leg irons shuffling past storefronts selling computer software, and veiled women walking the streets with new color television sets balanced on their heads."[1]

This contradiction illustrates the challenge Yemen faces. The country is caught between the tempting opportunities offered by imitating the West and the traditional values of the Islamic Middle East. Yemen knows it must please the West to attract investment and aid. At the same time, although many educated Yemenis want their country to modernize, they are reluctant to force people to give up traditional ways. If Yemen fails in this balancing act, the country may stagnate in poverty. But if it succeeds, Yemenis stand a good chance of finding peace and prosperity. Oil may help bring in the money needed to improve social programs. Tourism, shipping, and industry can be developed with the backing of foreign investment. Once again, Yemen will be able to take advantage of its location at the center of the world.

1

The Green Land of Arabia

Water is precious in Yemen, as it is throughout the Middle East, where vast, empty deserts dominate the landscape. Like its neighbors on the Arabian Peninsula, Yemen has no permanent rivers or lakes. Nevertheless, Yemen has a good supply of fresh water, thanks to rains that fall during the monsoon season. From April to August, summer winds blow in from the sea. As this moisture-laden air hits the mountains, it rises and cools. The moisture condenses into clouds and then falls as rain. This seasonal rain makes parts of Yemen good for farming and has given the country the nickname "Green Land of Arabia."

The monsoon winds enter Yemen from the Red Sea to the west and from the Gulf of Aden to the southeast. Inland from this long coastline, mountains rise, then drop down to deserts that stretch to Yemen's inland borders. Saudi Arabia meets Yemen's northern border, while Oman lies to the northeast. Yemen is at the southern end of the Arabian Peninsula, and indeed, its Arabic name, Al Yaman, comes from the word *yamanan*, meaning "south."

Yemen covers a total area of about 203,850 square miles (527,970 square kilometers), roughly the size of New York and California combined. Though not an especially large country, Yemen is geographically diverse. According to author/photographer Michael Jenner, "As one travels through the regions of Yemen, from the hot coastal plain of the Tihama to the cool mountain villages of the central highlands and to the remote valleys of the Hadramaut there is such a diversity of landscape, architecture, and vegetation that it is like moving from one country to another."[2]

The Islands

Yemen's diverse geography includes about 120 islands. Most of these lie off Yemen's western coast, in the Red Sea. However,

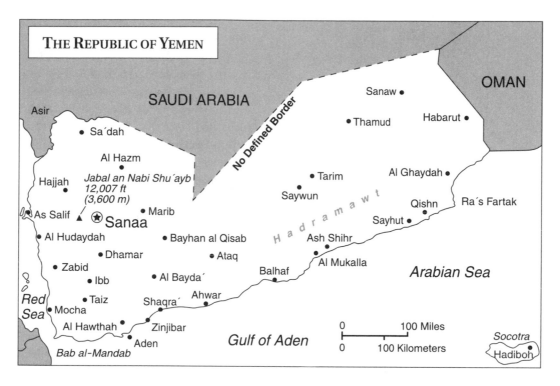

THE REPUBLIC OF YEMEN

SAUDI ARABIA

OMAN

Asir

Sanaw •

• Thamud   Habarut •

• Sa´dah

No Defined Border

Al Hazm

• Tarim   Al Ghaydah •

Jabal an Nabi Shu´ayb
12,007 ft
(3,600 m)

Hajjah

Saywun   Hadramawt

Qishn   Ra´s Fartak

As Salif   ⊛ Sanaa   • Marib

Sayhut •

• Al Hudaydah   • Bayhan al Qisab   Ash Shihr

• Dhamar   • Ataq   Al Mukalla

Red
Sea

• Zabid   Balhaf   Arabian Sea

• Ibb   • Al Bayda´

• Taiz   Ahwar

Mocha   Shaqra´

Al Hawthah   • Zinjibar   Gulf of Aden   0   100 Miles

Aden   0   100 Kilometers

Bab al-Mandab   Socotra

Hadiboh

Yemen's biggest island, Socotra, lies about 220 miles off the
southeast coast, in the Indian Ocean. Socotra covers about
fourteen hundred square miles, making it the largest island
in the Arab world. Historically, Socotra produced much of
the ancient world's frankincense, myrrh, and laudanum,
products that were used in religious ceremonies. Today the
islanders still harvest myrrh.

Because of the island's distance from the mainland, Socotra's residents were often isolated. Until the end of the twentieth century, Socotra had an airstrip suitable only for small
planes, which could not land during the blustery winds of
the monsoon season. During these four months each year,
the island's eighty thousand inhabitants were cut off from
outsiders and had to be completely self-sufficient. The first
tarmac airstrip in Socotra opened in 1999, and now jets make
two flights there most weeks, bringing supplies and tourists
to the island.

Two different ethnic groups live on Socotra. The people of
the mountains are thought to be the descendants of the orig-
inal population. They speak Soqotri, an old, unwritten language related to Arabic but quite different. They live in caves

and survive by farming and herding. Along the coast, the people are of mixed Arab, Portuguese, African, and Indian descent. They often speak Arabic as well as Soqotri. They live in stone huts and work mainly in fishing, trading, and herding cows, sheep, and goats. Socotra is the least developed part of Yemen, so the people there lack adequate schools, medical care, and job opportunities.

Though much smaller than Socotra, and almost uninhabited, Perim is perhaps Yemen's most important island. Perim lies two miles off the Yemeni coast in the middle of the straits of Bab al-Mandab, which link the Red Sea and the Gulf of Aden. Since all ships moving between the eastern Mediterranean and the Indian Ocean must pass through Bab al-Mandab, Perim helps give Yemen control over what today is one of the world's busiest shipping lanes.

ADEN: THE WORLD'S PORT

Many of the ships that pass through the straits of Bab al-Mandab stop at the city of Aden, in southern Yemen. The high mountains that circle Aden protect it from wind and storms, making the city ideal as a harbor. The mountains are the rim of an ancient volcano, no longer active, which left behind a dramatic landscape. A nineteenth-century traveler from Massachusetts, Joseph B.F. Osgood, described them as "sharp towering peaks, gothic spires, castellated ridges, and craggy masses overhanging awful precipices."[3]

For centuries Aden's status as an important trading center made the city a prime target for would-be conquerors, including the British, who held the city as a crown colony from 1839 to 1967. Many British ships stopped there for fuel during those years. By the end of that period, Aden was one of the world's largest ports, visited by about six thousand ships each year. But fewer ships stopped after the British left, and Aden's importance faded.

Today the Yemeni government is trying to make Aden an important center of trade once again. A $580 million project will expand the airport, improve docking for ships, and build warehouses, factories, and hotels. In addition, Aden is included in what the government has declared a free trade zone, which means that businesses there receive special tax breaks and other benefits. The government hopes that development will encourage more foreign ships to stop in

Aden. Already these measures have helped Aden to grow quickly. The economic opportunities have attracted immigrant workers from many countries, especially Somalia, India, Pakistan, and China. Together with the Yemeni Arabs, they make up a population of over half a million people.

THE TIHAMA: HOT EARTH

Aden lies along Yemen's coast in the area called the Tihama. This flat, narrow strip of land runs along the Red Sea and then turns east, continuing past the Gulf of Aden. This plain is hundreds of miles long but only fifteen to forty miles wide. It is bordered by high mountains on one side and water on the other.

The western part of the Tihama looks across the Red Sea to Africa. At the southernmost point of the Tihama, the

Cargo ships sail into Aden. The government has invested millions of dollars to make Aden an important center of trade.

African country of Djibouti is only twenty miles away across the straits of Bab al-Mandab. Over the centuries, many people have immigrated to the Tihama from African countries such as Djibouti and nearby Somalia. As a result, many Yemenis in the Tihama share cultural traits with their African neighbors. The immigration has continued in recent years, as refugees flee from war in Somalia.

The African settlers in Yemen have found that, like their homelands, the Tihama is hot and humid; in fact, the name Tihama means "hot earth." Temperatures there often rise over 100 degrees Fahrenheit during June and July. The traveler Osgood said of the coastal Tihama city of Mocha, "One is obliged to keep perfectly quiet at noon-day, with the mercury sometimes at the one hundred and twentieth degree, and hope that the heat may not increase a single degree for fear his body would actually melt."[4]

The Tihama's climate is made even harsher in July and August by sandstorms called *shamals*. High winds from the northwest pick up sand, dirt, and even chunks of clay. The debris whirls through the air for days, sometimes blocking out the sun. These sandstorms can destroy young crops, blow away good soil, and even take the paint off cars. So much gritty dirt can fill the air that airplanes are unable to fly, since debris would clog their engines.

Despite the destructive sandstorms, and a rainfall average of only four to eight inches per year, the Tihama is home to agriculture. Several major wadis, riverbeds that are dry for much of the year, carry monsoon rainwater that runs off from the mountains. In some parts of the foothills, these temporary rivers bring enough water to support four harvests each year. In addition, the high humidity means that when temperatures drop at night, dew forms, and this moisture helps plants grow. Thanks to the rain, the wadis, and the dew, the Tihama can produce many crops, including cotton, fruits, vegetables, and cereal crops such as millet and sorghum.

THE MOUNTAIN RANGES

Two major mountain chains rise above the Tihama. The western highlands run roughly north to south and contain many peaks that soar ten thousand feet or more. The highest mountain, Jabal an Nabi Shu'ayb (Prophet Shu'aib), reaches

12,012 feet, the highest point on the entire Arabian Peninsula. From the southern end of the western highlands, the central highlands run east along the coast. These mountains are lower, averaging less than thirty-three hundred feet. The entire L-shaped range is called Al-Sarat.

During most of the year, the mountains are cool and dry. The climate is mild except in winter, when temperatures can drop close to freezing and villagers wear heavy sheepskin jackets to protect themselves from the cold. Although winter may bring frosts at night, that is also the dry season, so Yemenis seldom see snow. In the summer, the monsoon rains wash over the mountains. Because the western mountains are higher, they trap more rain, so more people live and farm there. The highest peaks get up to thirty-five inches of rain per year, while the lower foothills get fifteen to twenty inches.

The rains that fall in the mountains provide water for people living on the plateaus that lie between the mountain peaks. Small villages have nestled in these fertile lands for centuries. Grains, coffee, mango, and papaya grow well in the western highlands. In the central highlands, where the lower mountains make for a drier and warmer climate, farmers favor peaches, apricots, almonds, and grapes.

Throughout the mountains, farmers make the best use of the land by cultivating even steep slopes. According to Michael Jenner, "The cultivation was made possible by mountain terracing. The last available scrap of land was carved from the mountainside and supported by a dry stone wall. This prevented not only erosion of the soil but also loss of surface water, which would otherwise have run away into the valley."[5] These terraces have been in use for perhaps fifteen hundred years. Unfortunately for the mountain farmers, centuries of irrigation have caused a buildup of mineral salts in the soil. The land has eroded as well and become more desertlike, so Yemen's mountain farms are not as productive as they once were.

Despite the less-fertile soil, most people in Yemen still live in these mountains, as their ancestors have done for generations. According to Yemeni scholar Dr. Yusuf Mohammed Abdullah, "Yemeni people feel secure in the mountains. They understand them. They know how to live with them and use them."[6]

In the mountainous regions of Yemen, farmers cultivate crops on terraced slopes.

Even though most people live in small mountain villages, a few towns have grown over the centuries into large cities. Yemen's capital and biggest city, Sanaa, sits in the western highlands. Sanaa is the oldest city in Yemen, and still contains many buildings that are hundreds of years old. Most of the city is modern, however; Sanaa has grown so rapidly in recent years that the city has enveloped nearby villages, and homes have emerged on what once was farmland. Sanaa's population has been doubling every four years since 1960. The city now has more than 1 million residents, and suffers from a great deal of noise and pollution as a consequence.

THE EASTERN DESERT

Fewer people live east of the mountains, where the foothills slope down gradually to meet the Eastern Desert. There is little to attract people to this region. The soil is dry and sandy, dust storms fill the air, sun scorches the land, and temperatures rise as high as 122 degrees Fahrenheit. The area receives little rainfall, so this is a desolate landscape, without many animals or plants.

Archaeologists speculate that this land was not always so barren, since ancient ruins suggest that large kingdoms once

GHUMDAN PALACE

The cities of Yemen feature many impressive buildings; in fact, Yemen has been famous for its works of architecture since ancient times. Legends tell of the beautiful Ghumdan Palace near Sanaa, built probably in the second century A.D. Poets and historians in ancient times praised the palace, making exaggerated claims, for example, that its shadow stretched ten miles and that its lights could be seen 750 miles away. The palace did reach ten to twenty stories, which was remarkable for that time. Supposedly, each of the palace's four sides was constructed of a different colored stone: red, green, white, and black. Bronze eagles and lions decorated its parapet; the beasts were hollow so that they seemed to screech and roar when the wind blew through them. The ceiling was made of alabaster stone so thin that one could see the crows flying overhead. In *Yemen: The Unknown Arabia*, Tim Mackintosh-Smith quotes the tenth-century Yemeni historian Al-Hamdani, who thought Ghumdan was near heaven:

> If Paradise's garden is above the skies,
> Then hard by heaven the roof of Ghumdan lies.
> And if God made on Earth a heaven for our eyes,
> Then Ghumdan's place is by that earthly paradise.

A pair of carved birds decorates a stone wall of the Ghumdan Palace.

flourished on the edge of the Eastern Desert. Today, however, only small, scattered villages break up the bleak landscape. Most of these villages are situated in the area's major wadis, such as the Wadi Hadramawt, where about two hundred thousand people live in scattered villages. The Wadi Hadramawt is a narrow valley about a mile wide, one hundred miles long, and one thousand feet deep. The name *Hadramawt* means "death is present," so named perhaps because people must struggle to survive in such a harsh climate. Nevertheless, a little rain, an average of two inches per year, falls in the wadi and allows the people to grow a few crops.

Dates are the most important crop in the Wadi Hadramawt; in fact, the valley is famous for them. Date palms can grow in this dry region because they do not depend on rainfall. Instead, their deep roots pull in moisture trapped far below the ground. Date palms can grow over ninety feet tall, and each tree produces thousands of dates every year. The dates last a long time when dried, and they are high in calories, which is important when food is scarce. The date palms also provide wood for building and furniture, and their leaves can be woven into baskets.

THE ARAB IDEAL

Though the Bedouin make up only a small percentage of Yemen's population, they were often seen as the ideal Arab. According to the book *Aramco and Its World*, "To settled Arabs, the Bedouins have traditionally been regarded as the repositories of manly virtues: they were proud, independent, resourceful, courageous, loyal, hospitable, and generous. In addition, they were thought to speak the purest Arabic, uncontaminated by contact with foreign elements in the cities."

Though widely admired, these nomads did not have easy lives in the harsh desert. They had to find water not only for themselves, but also for their herds of camels, horses, and goats, which they kept mainly for milk. In the past, Bedouin tribes divided much of the Arabian Peninsula into tribal ranges, each with its own wells. No one could use another tribe's well or cross another tribe's land without permission, and when water was particularly scarce, a tribe might start a war by trying to take over another tribe's well.

North of the Wadi Hadramawt, along the border with Saudi Arabia, Yemen's Eastern Desert meets the vast Arabian Desert. This area is called the Rub al-Khali, or Empty Quarter. The entire desert, including the parts in Saudi Arabia and Oman, is the largest continuous body of sand in the world, 750 miles long and up to 400 miles wide. This is also one of the world's hottest and emptiest sand-dune deserts. The Empty Quarter may not see rain for five years at a time, so farming there is impossible. Yet even in this desolate landscape, water is available at a few scattered oases, so bands of Bedouin nomads are able to live in the desert. They travel between the oases to find enough water for their cattle, sheep, and goats.

In the 1980s, geologists discovered a natural resource in the Empty Quarter that to the industrial world is even more valuable than water: oil. Yemen began exporting oil in 1987, and several foreign companies are now exploring or drilling for oil in the desert. Yemen already produces nearly half a million barrels of oil per day, worth more than $1 billion (U.S.) each year. Yemen also plans to develop the natural gas fields that are associated with oil wells. Yemen's government hopes that the oil and natural gas reserves will fuel the country's development for many years. With the money from oil, Yemen's people can buy many of the goods their own country cannot produce.

PLANTS AND ANIMALS

The diversity of Yemen's geography results in great diversity among the country's plants and animals. Yemen is home to hundreds of plant species, including many found nowhere else. Socotra alone has more than eight hundred plant species, and at least three hundred of those are endemic—that is, they are found nowhere else. These include the desert rose and the cucumber tree, the only variety of cucumber that grows as a tree.

Many of Yemen's endemic species are threatened by human activity, such as development and livestock grazing. On Socotra Island, for example, many of the rare plants are in danger of extinction. The government's conservation policies can be contradictory, however. For example, Yemen's tourism bureau calls Socotra "the last refuge of the almost extinct," but at the same time it is building luxury hotels to attract tourists.

An oil refinery stretches across the Yemeni desert. Oil production provides vital revenue for Yemen.

The challenge will be to develop economic opportunities and social services for the island's residents while still protecting the natural habitat. Henri Dumont, in the book *Soqotra*, asks, "Will the backbone of Soqotra's fragile ecosystem break under the weight of a sudden invasion of 20th century technology and consumerism, or will it be able to maintain its status of a unique natural monument, jealously guarded and protected by the Yemeni government, with support from the United Nations and its various agencies?"[7] The next few years will provide the answers.

Yemen's diversity also extends to birds, some of which are unique to small regions within Yemen. Socotra Island alone has about 150 bird species. Seventeen bird species are native to Yemen. Most of these live in the mountains, including unique species of partridge, warbler, woodpecker, and thrush. The seacoasts are home to seabirds and waders, including pink-backed pelicans, reef herons, and spoonbills; flocks of the native Arabian golden sparrow live on the coastal plains of the Tihama. The farmlands of the Tihama are also home to the Arabian bustard, Yemen's largest bird at three feet tall. Although found elsewhere, its population in

Yemen is important to the survival of this rare bird. More common bird species include sparrows, pigeons, and starlings. In addition to the birds that live in Yemen year-round, about 350 bird species stop in Yemen during their migrations between Asia and Europe.

Yemen has fewer endemic animal than bird species, but it is home to two species of rare baboons. One of these, the gelada baboon, is Yemen's largest wild mammal. Gelada baboons are distinctive for the hourglass-shaped patch of bright pink skin they have on their chests. They usually live in groups in Yemen's northwestern mountains. Hamadryas baboons also live in the mountains, usually in groups of twenty to fifty. The mountains offer both baboon species a variety of wild foods, as well as refuge in secluded gullies far from human development.

Socotra has several rare reptiles, such as the Socotra Island blind snake and the Socotra leaf-toed gecko. Yemen's other

Socotra Island's endemic Dragon's Blood trees provide food and habitat for a diverse bird population.

wild animals include wolves, hyenas, foxes, porcupines, and hares. Dozens of bat and rodent species also live throughout Yemen. Yemen at one time had wild pumas, leopards, giraffes, ibex, and oryx, but these animals disappeared over the course of the twentieth century, driven to extinction either by hunting or by loss of their natural habitat to human encroachment. Today a few of these species survive in Yemen's zoos, and there have been some unconfirmed reports of wild leopards.

NOT AN EASY LIFE

The Green Land of Arabia stands out among Middle Eastern countries for its fertile regions washed by seasonal rainfall. Yet life is not easy for the people of Yemen. Farmers must work hard to grow crops on steep mountain slopes or in sandy soil. The population is growing rapidly, and agricultural production cannot keep pace. The land holds few natural resources besides oil, and the development of that industry is still in its infancy.

The people of Yemen have a long history of overcoming challenges, however. They have learned to make good use of their land and to make the most of their location along the Gulf of Aden and the Red Sea. To prosper, they must continue to take advantage of their country's resources. Most Yemenis are anxious to benefit from the opportunities and conveniences enjoyed by modern industrial nations. They know, moreover, that their country was once an important player in the ancient world, and hope it can be so again.

Occupations and Independence

The monsoon winds that brought rain to southern Arabia, what today is Yemen, also brought with them ships loaded with trade goods. As far back as 1000 B.C., ships came to southern Arabia from China, India, and Africa. Many of these ships left their merchandise in Yemen, where it was loaded aboard camels for the journey north and west to the Mediterranean. The ancient Greeks and Romans thought that all the rich trade items came directly from Yemen itself. They called the country "Happy Arabia" because they saw it as a land of plenty. Still, even though Yemen did not produce all the goods that passed through it, the country benefited from the trade.

Desert Communities

In the earliest days of civilization in Yemen, communities flourished around the Eastern Desert by making the best use of potential farmland. City-states developed and sponsored the building of huge dams and irrigation systems that allowed people to farm dry areas. For example, scholars believe that the Marib Dam in the kingdom of Saba may have irrigated enough farmland to feed three hundred thousand people. According to the book *Aramco and Its World*, "Nearly two thousand feet across, the dam spanned the Wadi Adhanah in the black hills near Marib, the capital of Saba, deflecting and retaining the waters of seasonal flash floods, and, through an elaborate system of sluices and canals, distributing the water to the cultivated areas."[8] Agriculture fed the people, and trade allowed these cities to prosper.

By about 1000 B.C., southern Arabia was dominated by a handful of city-states, which prospered because they were major stops on trade routes across the ancient world. Ships brought silk from China; spices and cloth from India; and

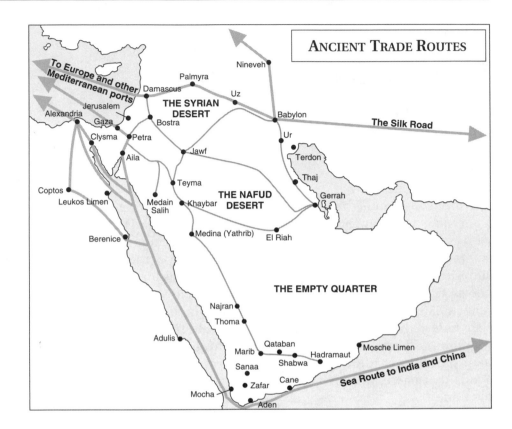

ANCIENT TRADE ROUTES

To Europe and other Mediterranean ports

Nineveh

Palmyra
Damascus
Uz
THE SYRIAN DESERT
Jerusalem
Alexandria
Gaza
Bostra
Clysma
Petra
Aila
Jawf
Babylon
The Silk Road
Ur
Terdon
Thaj
Teyma
Coptos
Leukos Limen
Medain Salih
Khaybar
THE NAFUD DESERT
Gerrah
Berenice
Medina (Yathrib)
El Riah

THE EMPTY QUARTER

Najran
Thoma
Adulis
Qataban
Marib
Hadramaut
Mosche Limen
Sanaa
Shabwa
Cane
Sea Route to India and China
Mocha
Zafar
Aden

gold, ivory, and slaves from Africa. Caravans up to twenty miles long with three thousand camels then carried these goods across the Arabian Peninsula. Merchants traded with Mesopotamia and Babylon in what is today Iraq; with Egypt, Syria, and Palestine; and with the countries around the Mediterranean Sea. Merchants who passed through Yemen had to pay a tax to each city they visited, thus leaving a little of their wealth behind.

In addition to collecting taxes, the people of southern Arabia prospered from the sale of two valuable local resources. The resins frankincense and myrrh come from trees that grow only in southern Arabia and northeastern Africa. Michael Jenner explains that "the aromatic gums were precious commodities throughout the ancient world. Their uses extended from medicine and cosmetics to food flavouring and chewing gum."[9] Pliny, a Roman writer from the first century A.D., wrote, "Frankincense after being collected is conveyed to [the city of] Sabota on camels, one of the gates of the city being opened for its admission; the kings have made it a capital offence for camels so laden to turn aside from the high road. At Sabota a tithe [tax of 10 percent]…is taken by the priests.…The journey is divided into 65 stages with halts for camels."[10]

For over a thousand years the kingdoms of southern Arabia participated in a booming trade. Yet despite the great wealth of southern Arabia, all that Europeans knew about the mysterious region was rumors—for example, that winged serpents guarded the frankincense trees. The ancient Greek geographer and historian Strabo wrote that the people of southern Arabia had "a great quantity of articles wrought in gold and silver, as couches, tripods, basins, drinking vessels, to which we must add the costly magnificence of their houses for the doors, walls and roofs are variegated with inlaid ivory, gold, silver and precious stones."[11] Although the homes of the wealthiest citizens may have been furnished that lavishly, scholars believe that most people probably lived modestly and that life was harder than Strabo's description might suggest. Many citizens would have had to work hard to maintain the irrigation systems and to grow enough food for everyone in that dry environment.

THE FADING OF TRADE AND GODS

What Strabo and other Westerners seemed unaware of—and the people of southern Arabia kept secret—was their knowledge of the monsoon winds that propelled ships to China and India. That secret was the key to the region's prosperity. As long as Western countries did not know how to reach these Eastern lands, all trade between East and West had to pass through Arabia.

The Arabian kingdoms could not keep their monsoons secret forever. In the first century A.D., a Mediterranean sailor named Hippalus learned about the monsoon winds. "Let the summer monsoon blow the ships south of the Red Sea and all the way east to India, and the winter monsoon bring them back,"[12] he said. After this discovery, the Greeks and Romans traveled the entire trade routes in their own ships. The inland caravan routes fell into disuse, and the Arabian kingdoms faded in importance. Trade shifted west to Yemen's coast, where ships could stop for fuel before continuing their journey. This new trade route brought prosperity to the kingdom of Himyar on the Red Sea coast. By A.D. 50 the Himyarites controlled southwestern Arabia and the shipping lanes through the straits of Bab al-Mandab.

In the centuries that followed, changes occurred that brought conflict to southern Arabia. The people of the eastern kingdoms had worshiped many gods, particularly those associated with the sun, moon, and morning star. Then, in the fourth and fifth centuries A.D., Jewish and Christian missionaries brought their worship of a single god (monotheism) to Arabia. Conflict came with the new beliefs, however. For example, in the early sixth century the Himyarite king Dhu Nawas is said to have converted to Judaism and ordered all his people to do the same. In his zeal, Dhu Nawas executed more than twenty thousand Christians who refused. In response, the Christian king of Ethiopia, Abraha, invaded Yemen in 525 and held the region for almost fifty years.

When the Ethiopian king died, the Himyarites rebelled. They asked for help from the Persians, who ruled an empire centered in what is now Iran. According to scholar Robin Bidwell, a Himyarite prince convinced the Persian emperor to help by claiming that Yemen held valuable minerals: "[The prince] was given an army, consisting entirely of criminals released from jail, with the idea that if they succeeded, Persia would gain a new province; whereas if they failed their loss would hardly matter."[13] The Himyarites and their motley helpers defeated the Ethiopians in 575. The Himyarites had little time to celebrate, however, before Persia took control of the southern Arabian kingdoms.

The great days of "Happy Arabia" were at an end. Yemen had lost its independence. In addition, as Christianity spread, demand for frankincense and myrrh, which had brought southern Arabia much wealth, dropped, since Christians did not use these substances in their funeral rituals. The weakened eastern kingdoms decayed even further. The Marib Dam was neglected and broke several times. After the dam collapsed in 570, people deserted the area. As Jenner notes, "Thus more than one thousand years of developed civilisation came to an end. The very settlements were abandoned as the people drifted off either into a primitive nomadic existence or trekked into the mountains to carve small fields out of the slopes by the use of stone terracing."[14]

YEMENI JEWS

Few Jews live in Yemen today, but Judaism has an ancient history there. Jews have lived in Yemen since at least the fourth century A.D. Though Christianity was outlawed around 630, when Islam became the country's official religion, Judaism remained. In the eighteenth century, some two thousand Jews lived at Sanaa, where they were known for their work in gold and silver. They lived outside the city in a separate village and were not allowed to spend the night in Sanaa or to carry weapons. According to a European visitor, the imam (ruler) treated the Jews with contempt but protected them in exchange for a small yearly tribute.

After the nation of Israel was established in 1948, the Israelis organized a program, called Operation Magic Carpet, to bring Yemeni Jews to Israel, and some fifty thousand Jews left Yemen. The few thousand Jews remaining in Yemen were scattered across the country, but they still maintained their religion. In *Motoring with Mohammed*, Eric Hansen quoted an Orthodox rabbi from Brooklyn. In the 1980s, this rabbi brought religious texts to Jews in Yemen's remote mountain villages. "Yemeni society is tolerant," the rabbi said. "The situation here demonstrates how well Jews and Moslems can live together without the interference of Zionism and Israel. Yemeni Jews are very orthodox, but they also chew *qat* (a narcotic plant) with their Moslem neighbors."

After Yemeni reunification in 1990, Jewish groups in Israel and the United States convinced many more Yemeni Jews to leave Yemen. Only a few hundred Jews remain in Yemen today.

A Jewish Yemeni family smiles for the camera. Most Jews have left Yemen for a life in Israel.

ISLAMIC INFLUENCE

Southern Arabia had fallen into political and religious disunity. Before long, however, Judaism and Christianity were pushed aside by a new religion on the Arabian Peninsula. In about 610, an Arab merchant named Muhammad began to have visions, which became the basis of Islam. Muhammad's new faith quickly spread through the Arabian Peninsula. The Persian governor of Yemen converted to Islam in 628, and the rest of Yemen soon followed. As their leaders converted, whole tribes followed their example. Thousands of new disciples then joined the Islamic armies that set out to spread the faith by conquering new territory.

The Arabian tribes had always been ferociously independent; Islam helped to give them a sense of unity. As Jenner explains, "The word of Allah…ordains not just religion but every aspect of social, economic and political life. Submission to the word of Allah therefore implies the adopting of a complete way of life which aims to unite mankind in a universal Muslim brotherhood."[15]

The crumbling walls of the Marib Dam serve as testament to the ingenuity of Yemen's ancient cultures.

The unity that Islam brought to the Arabian Peninsula did not last. When Muhammad died, his followers disagreed about who their next leader should be, and Islam split into two sects. On the one hand, Sunnis elected their religious leader, called a caliph (literally "successor"), from all qualified male Muslims. Shiites, on the other hand, chose their leader only from the descendants of Muhammad's son-in-law, Ali. Smaller branches eventually split from each of these groups. Eventually, although most people of southern Arabia followed Islam, they interpreted the religion in different ways. One of the most influential groups was the Zaydis, a Shiite sect. The Zaydis would control parts of Yemen for over a thousand years.

Under Islam, the Arabian Peninsula once again prospered. According to Bidwell, "despite intermittent strife between groups of its people, life in mediaeval Yemen was as rich and as cultured as anywhere in the contemporary world."[16] Long camel caravans once more crossed the land. This time they brought pilgrims up the Red Sea coast to Mecca, Islam's holy city. The caravans traveled in the cool of night, led by advance guards carrying torches. The caravan typically included soldiers, a chef with a staff of cooks, doctors, musicians, a judge, and other officials. One camel might carry an elaborate silk-covered litter with a gorgeously decorated Koran (the Muslim holy book) as a gift to Mecca.

The Zaydis were never able to unite Yemen completely, however. The coastal areas were relatively stable and prosperous, but in the mountains violence between tribes often erupted over political and religious differences. In the tenth century, Yemen contained at least four independent kingdoms that fought with each other. Fighting between the various kingdoms and tribes exhausted and weakened Yemen, leaving the country vulnerable to foreign attack.

OUTSIDE INTEREST

Despite the discord, trade between the Mediterranean and the Far East still passed through the Red Sea and the straits of Bab al-Mandab, and this fact made Yemen a tempting target for would-be conquerors. In the sixteenth century, several European countries wanted to control that trade route. Portugal, for example, took over the island of Socotra in 1507, but quickly realized that Aden was the key to control of the

Red Sea. Bidwell describes the attack led by Portuguese commander Afonso de Albuquerque:

> He had a friendly reception from the Governor [the ruler of Aden], who sent fowls, sheep, lemons and oranges and offered to surrender the town, but de Albuquerque preferred his usual policy of obtaining submission by force....He decided upon a direct assault on the strong sea walls. Specially built scaling ladders...were erected, and some soldiers penetrated the town before the ladders broke under the weight of armoured men.[17]

After this failed strategy, Albuquerque set up a base on a Red Sea island, where many of his men died of fever. Over the next few years, the governor of Aden agreed three more times to become a vassal of Portugal. The Portuguese never stayed in the city to enforce their rule, however, and the governor ignored his promise as soon as they left.

Despite its failure, Albuquerque's attack worried Egypt, which wanted the straits open for its own use. Egypt sent a fleet to take control of the area. In 1515 Egypt seized much of the Tihama and the mountains around Sanaa, but it, too, failed to conquer Aden.

Aden could not stand against the next invaders, however. The Ottoman Empire, a Muslim kingdom ruled from Turkey, had the most powerful military in the region. The Ottomans conquered Egypt in 1517 and then invaded the Arabian Peninsula. The Ottoman Turks used Egyptian soldiers to subdue the Yemenis in a long, bloody war. A brutal but clever Ottoman slave captured Aden at last, through treachery, as Bidwell explains: "When his fleet put into Aden, he [the slave] invited the Tahirid Sultan on board and hanged him from the yardarm. Simultaneously, Turkish soldiers who had been sent ashore on stretchers, allegedly for medical treatment, rose up and seized the fortifications."[18] By 1585 the Ottomans had most of Yemen under their control, though they never entirely subdued the Zaydis.

The Ottomans lived richly in Yemen. Visitors to Sanaa described beautiful gardens and orchards, splendid mosques, luxurious public baths, richly dressed noblemen, and tame leopards that were kept as pets. In many ways the Yemeni people also benefited from Ottoman rule, since they were

ZABID UNIVERSITY

In the ninth century, an Islamic governor named Ibn Ziyad founded the town of Zabid, in the Tihama. He turned a famous mosque there into Zabid University, which became one of the world's most important centers for Sunni teaching for hundreds of years. At Zabid's height, thousands of students from Yemen and other countries studied at the town's two hundred schools. Islamic law was the main course of study, but students could also study Arabic grammar, history, poetry, and math. It is believed that the university operated as late as the eighteenth century. Today several independent schools that teach the Koran remain.

The mosque in Zabid became a center of learning in ancient Yemen.

now part of a large kingdom with its extensive trade network. Yemen's trade with Europe grew, especially after Europeans were introduced to coffee, which was made from the beans of a plant that grew in Yemen's mountains. The Dutch, French, and English set up coffee factories in the port of Mocha, which became the center of worldwide coffee trade. Once again, ships from many nations stopped at Yemen's shores.

LOCAL RULE AT LAST

Despite the advantages of Ottoman rule, the Yemenis resented being controlled by foreigners. Many tribes rebelled, with little success. Then a twenty-year-old Zaydi named Qasim led a resistance movement against the Turks. His exploits are legendary: Qasim escaped his enemies by hiding in a tree, he disguised himself as an Indian, and his warriors fought with stones and won against Turkish muskets. In many ways his achievements were typical of his Zaydi ancestors. According to Bidwell, "Once again the chroniclers recount the miraculous powers, the ostentatious simplicity of life, the rigid enforcement of religious law…and the meticulous collection of taxes for distribution to the poor."[19]

Qasim's rebellion united people throughout the region against the Ottomans. He controlled the area north of Sanaa by 1607, and the Turks agreed to let him rule there. Qasim's son, Muayyad Mohammed, began fighting again in 1629 and ousted the Turks from Yemen entirely in 1636.

The Zaydis then set out to expand their empire by conquering other tribes. By 1658 they controlled all of what is today Yemen. Under Zaydi rule, the country continued to prosper and to awe the few Europeans who saw it. Bidwell writes that one eighteenth-century explorer "considered

A view of the historic section of Sanaa reveals the architectural splendor of Yemen's capital.

Sanaa a paradise, with its courteous and hospitable inhabitants, its *suq* [market] filled with goods from Europe and India and its magnificent buildings both public and private."[20]

The coffee trade also boomed, with several European companies active in Mocha. In 1720, Yemen produced most of the world's coffee, and the country could hardly keep up with the demand. Yemen's control of the trade did not last, however. Someone smuggled the coffee plant out of Yemen and started new plantations in places such as Indonesia and Brazil, where the coffee plants thrived. After 1740, Yemen lost its hold on the coffee trade, and the country's income dropped.

At the same time, the Zaydis' power weakened. Tribes from Saudi Arabia raided the Tihama and destroyed many villages. Yemeni tribes also rebelled, and the Zaydis lost control of several regions. In the southwest, the sultan of Lahej declared himself an independent ruler. He kept the Zaydis out of Aden after 1728, starting a division between northern and southern Yemen that would last for more than 250 years. The Zaydis' empire dissolved into independent warring tribes.

A BRITISH CROWN COLONY

Once again, a foreign power was ready to take advantage of Yemen's weakness. The British East India Company traded between Europe and India, and the company's ships often stopped in Aden for supplies. The British, in order to eliminate the threat of a French invasion of India, took over the island of Perim in 1799. This move gave Britain control of the straits of Bab al-Mandab, through which French ships bound for India would have to move. Even after the French threat to India ended, the British considered the Turks to be a threat to British shipping. They determined, therefore, to set up a base to protect and supply British ships.

The British moved to Aden, where the sultan of Lahej welcomed them as guests. The British, however, wanted to take complete control of the city, and soon they found an excuse to do just that. A ship flying British flags was wrecked near Aden, and local people plundered the ship. The sultan denied knowledge of the robbery, but the British found the ship's goods for sale in the sultan's own warehouse. The British demanded compensation. In 1838 the sultan agreed to sell Aden to the British. The two sides were unable to agree on the terms, however, and the next year Britain took the city by force.

All this effort was for control of a town with about six hundred people, living in some ninety run-down stone buildings. The British commander Stafford Bettesworth Haines claimed of Aden that "its trade is annihilated, its governor imbecile, its [water] tanks in ruins, its water half-brackish, with deserted streets and still more deserted ports."[21] Yet Haines saw the city's potential as a center of trade as well as a military base. Shipping increased after 1869, when the Suez Canal, an artificial waterway connecting the Mediterranean and Red Seas, opened. Aden's importance as a coaling station for steamships grew, and it became one of the world's busiest ports. Within a few years the population grew to over twenty thousand.

In order to protect their new Arabian colony, the British signed many friendship treaties with neighboring tribes. The local tribal leaders, or sheikhs, promised that they would not sell or give away any land without British approval. In return, the sheikhs received money and gifts from the British. The British also promised to protect the tribes from the Ottoman Turks.

THE OTTOMAN OCCUPATION ... AGAIN

Britain focused its attention on the tribes closest to Aden, and did not enter into treaties with tribes farther north. Northern Yemen, therefore, was more vulnerable to the Ottoman Turks, who claimed all Muslim lands as theirs. The Turks took advantage of Yemen's chaotic politics, since many tribal leaders were fighting for dominance. They seized control of the northern Tihama region in 1849. From there they moved into the mountains and captured Sanaa in 1871.

Despite their successes, the Turks did not find Yemen easy to control. The people of Yemen refused to accept the Ottoman claim to all Muslim lands. The Yemenis were particularly offended when the Ottomans replaced traditional Islamic law with a new code based on Western legal principles. Local sheikhs rebelled against Ottoman rule; meanwhile, a few mountain strongholds were never conquered by the Turks.

Even as the tribes of northern Yemen fought the Turks, they fought each other. What they needed was a strong leader to unite them against their invaders. They finally found one in 1891, when a Muslim preacher named Muhammad ibn Yahya became the Zaydi imam, or religious leader. He accepted the Ottomans' right to lead the Islamic world in dealing with foreigners, but the imam demanded that he be allowed to rule local religious affairs, which included enforcing laws and collecting taxes. Yemenis rallied behind him and started a coordinated rebellion. His son, Yahya ibn Mohammed, took over leadership in 1904 and attacked the

TRIBAL JUSTICE

Each Yemeni tribe is led by a sheikh, who is both a leader and a judge. The sheikh entertains visitors on the tribe's behalf, protects the tribe's allies, and supervises group work. According to photojournalist Pascal Maréchaux, in *Arabia Felix*, "Elected by his kinsmen, it is [the sheikh's] task to maintain law and order in these villages…The influence he wields is a function of his charisma and diplomacy, and the skill he has shown in reconciling opposing parties." In some villages, Maréchaux adds, "When a dispute arises between two men, each gives his *djambia* [dagger] to the sheikh, symbolically asking him to defend his interests. By handing over his weapon, a man implies that he will not take the law into his own hands, and he pledges his honour to abide by the verdict."

Yemeni tribal members escort their sheikh (in white) to ensure his safety.

Turks in Sanaa. The Ottomans sent thousands of soldiers into Yemen, but still the tribes stormed Turkish forts or besieged them until starvation forced the Turks to surrender.

Meanwhile, the British held on to Aden. They signed more friendship treaties with surrounding tribes in order to have a buffer between themselves and the Ottomans. After many small skirmishes and arguments, the British and Ottomans finally agreed to divide Yemen between them. In 1905 they drew a border between British control in the south and the region the Ottomans claimed in the north.

The British may have accepted Turkish rule in the north, but the northern Yemenis did not. Yahya ibn Mohammed continued his resistance movement and in 1911 the Ottomans signed a peace agreement that gave him control over most of northern Yemen. The Turks still held the Tihama, but they lost even that in 1918, under terms of the treaty that ended World War I and required the Turks to withdraw entirely from Yemen. Other nations recognized northern Yemen as an independent country, with Yahya as its king. Southern Yemen became a British protectorate, with Yemenis ruling locally but Britain handling international affairs.

Peace briefly settled on Yemen, though the country was divided. The future would bring more revolutions and more change. Throughout the chaos, people in both North and South Yemen would yearn for the day when they might again be united as a single nation.

Chapter opening

North and South Fight and Unite

Throughout most of its history, Yemen was not really a single country at all but, rather, a collection of tribes or kingdoms seeking to dominate their neighbors. In the twentieth century, both North and South Yemen fought for independence and reform. Although the two Yemens dreamed of uniting into one country, for many years they only grew further apart politically. They would not realize their dream of unification until near the end of the twentieth century.

To Rule Greater Yemen

Imam Yahya wanted to rule "Greater Yemen," both North and South, the land of the ancient Himyarites and of Qasim the Great. Many tribes, however, no longer saw the need for unified rule once they had won independence from the Turks. Throughout the region, local leaders fought each other for power. Even some Zaydi tribes refused to support Yahya. Saudi Arabia, with the backing of some Yemeni tribes, invaded the northwest. Meanwhile, British troops tried to take back the territory they had earlier lost to the Turks. The British were also afraid that Imam Yahya would try to force them from the country, so they gave weapons to tribal leaders fighting against the imam.

In an effort to force cooperation from the tribes, Yahya's soldiers took tribal leaders hostage. Sheikhs were sent in chains to Sanaa, where some spent years in Yahya's dungeons. The battle to subdue the northern tribes used up most of his energy, so finally Yahya gave up on getting the British out of South Yemen. In 1934 Yahya and Britain signed a treaty that kept the old British-Turkish border between North and South. Soon after, Yahya and Saudi Arabia agreed to a boundary between them. Although Yahya never officially gave up his claims to Greater Yemen, after 1934 he stayed in North Yemen.

Imam Yahya's summer palace perches atop a sandstone pinnacle. Yahya was determined to rid North Yemen of foreign control.

KEEPING THE WORLD OUT

Yahya was determined that foreign powers would not influence North Yemen. In his view, other countries in the region had lost their freedom because they had let Westerners develop and control their resources. Anthropologist Paul Dresch points out that "immediately after World War I the Imam was the only Arab ruler not either under Western control or at least on a Western payroll."[22]

Yahya was willing to trade prosperity for his nation's independence. He declared, "I would rather that my people and I eat straw than let foreigners in."[23] Yahya kept the country isolated from the rest of the world, and tried to control trade through a government monopoly. Yahya did encourage some forms of modernization, though. He established a full-time army, instead of just calling on the tribes to send fighters when he needed them. He invited learned men from throughout the Islamic world to visit and sent people to Iraq to gain technical skills and military training. He also promoted schools for clerks, judges, and teachers. However, these schools taught mostly religion and religious law, generally ignoring modern science and business. As a result, North Yemen stagnated economically. Yemen had no factories or paved roads and few schools or doctors.

Yahya found that he had to modify his observance of Islamic principles in order to solve some of the government's problems. For example, to cover government expenses, the imam imposed road tolls and customs taxes, in spite of Islam's prohibition of most taxes. Yahya's ideals also could not prevent a series of droughts and famines. Food shortages and high taxes forced many North Yemenis to emigrate to other countries. Young men moved to South Yemen, to Africa, and even to Britain, America, Indonesia, and Vietnam. By the mid-1940s, some 750,000 North Yemenis were living in foreign countries.

Across Yemen, people wanted change. Young Yemenis educated abroad returned to see how poor and undeveloped their country was; they wanted the opportunities and comforts they had seen elsewhere. Merchants resented the government's control of trade. Soldiers were unhappy with their pay and

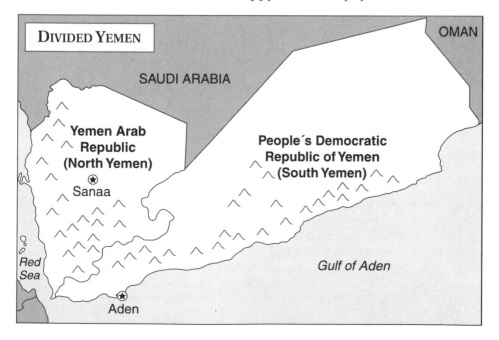

DIVIDED YEMEN

OMAN

SAUDI ARABIA

Yemen Arab
Republic
(North Yemen)

⊛
Sanaa

People's Democratic
Republic of Yemen
(South Yemen)

Red
Sea

Gulf of Aden

⊛
Aden

believed that the imam was hiding great wealth for his own use. Zaydi religious leaders were disturbed that Yahya planned for his oldest son to succeed him; their policy was to elect the imam from all qualified men. Other tribes resented having a Zaydi king and wanted to rule their own territory independently.

FREE YEMEN!

As discontent rose, people began to talk of rebellion. A group of intellectuals formed the Free Yemen Movement (FYM) to push for government reforms, as well as better roads, schools, and hospitals. Students, farmers, and laborers formed other groups advocating change. When Imam Yahya learned of these movements, he had many reformers jailed or exiled.

LIFE UNDER IMAM YAHYA

Life was hard in North Yemen during the reign of Imam Yahya. Most northerners were poor farmers who lived on bread and porridge. Villagers lived with dirt, fleas, and the smoke of oil lamps. Half the children died at birth or soon after, women spent hours hauling foul water from distant cisterns, and men fought constant gun battles with each other. Smallpox killed or blinded thousands, and swarms of locusts destroyed entire crops.

Even the imam lived simply and worked hard. Imam Yahya paid great attention to small details and closely supervised the business of government. In the early years, he dealt with all complaints himself. An account from 1922, quoted in *A History of Modern Yemen* by Paul Dresch, describes the imam's workday: "Every letter written, no matter how unimportant, is placed before the Couch of State and [Imam Yahya], after reading it and adding a word at the end in his own hand…gives it to the soldier before him….About midnight, the telegraph clerk comes with a packet of telegrams. …The Imam and the First Secretary remain sometimes until the early dawn."

Even if the North Yemenis lived poorly, at least they knew their leader was working hard on their behalf. Later, as his health was failing and the government grew more complex, Imam Yahya delegated more authority to local governors. Without his direct control, corruption and bribery grew, and the lives of ordinary people got even worse.

Despite the imam's opposition, Yahya's oldest son, Ahmad, befriended several members of the FYM. For a while he showed interest in their ideas for reform, and the FYM hoped that Ahmad might one day rule North Yemen and make positive changes. But after an argument in 1944, Ahmad turned against the FYM and declared, "I pray God I do not die before I color my sword here with the blood of these modernists."[24] The reformers fled to Aden, where they started planning a revolution. They hoped to unite North and South Yemen under a modern constitution. An imam would still rule as a figurehead, but the real power would lie in the hands of a parliament.

The FYM started the rebellion on February 17, 1948, by assassinating Imam Yahya. They also tried but failed to kill Ahmad, who called the northern tribes to defend him. Most Yemenis knew nothing of the reformers' plans and were shocked by the murder of the imam. The tribes rallied around Ahmad and crushed the revolution in less than a month. Hundreds of reformers were jailed, and many leaders were executed. Ahmad released most of the surviving rebels within a few years, and North Yemen's politics stabilized. Reform groups still pressed for change, but since they disagreed on their specific goals, the groups remained small and did not develop any real power.

LIKE FATHER, LIKE SON

In some ways Ahmad broke with his father's policies. He accepted some foreign aid to start a few development programs. Foreigners entered Yemen as diplomats, military trainers, and economic advisers. But in general, according to scholar Robin Bidwell, Ahmad "ruled much as Yahya had done, showing the same enormous knowledge and intuitive understanding of the country, the same careful attention to the welfare, particularly the spiritual welfare, of his people, and the same harsh repression when it appeared necessary."[25]

North Yemen remained poor, isolated, and underdeveloped. The country had one bank and no industry except for one unprofitable textile factory. No girls went to school, and boys studied only Islam and classical texts. Few people had electricity, safe drinking water, or sewage systems. Most people could not get medical care, and 80 percent of the population suffered from the eye disease trachoma. The government was slow to accomplish anything. Ahmad had to personally approve every action, down to the feeding of mules or the purchase of inkwells for a school. Yet he would spend days at a time in fasting and prayer, ignoring all government work while the country stagnated. According to guidebook author Pertti Hamalainen, "In 1962, Yemen was probably the most medieval country in the world."[26]

People throughout North Yemen were unhappy. Peasants struggled against poverty. Soldiers who had not been paid rioted. Thousands of Yemenis found work abroad, and communities of liberal North Yemenis flourished in Aden and in Cairo, Egypt. Their views reached deep into Yemen's mountains through radio broadcasts from Egypt.

CIVIL WAR

The modern age finally entered Yemen after Ahmad's death in 1962. His son, Mohammed al-Badr, became imam. Though he promised many reforms, Badr was known to be a heavy drinker and was generally seen as incompetent. After only a few days, a group of army officers overthrew Badr and founded the Yemen Arab Republic (YAR). The new government promised social justice, education for everyone, and adherence to Islamic law. The new leaders also backed Arab nationalism, the idea that the Arab world should unite into a single state and eliminate all Western influence. Egypt, a major supporter of Arab nationalism, sent advisers and soldiers to help the YAR rebellion.

Most of the world welcomed the new government, and in 1963 YAR joined the United Nations. At home, however, the nation's leaders struggled for control. Many tribes resented the presence of Egyptian soldiers and saw the republican government as a puppet of Egypt. They offered support to Badr instead, in hopes of bringing back the traditional rule of imams.

Some foreign powers were worried, too. The royal family of Saudi Arabia was afraid that a successful rebellion in Yemen might inspire Saudis to rebel against their monarch. Britain was afraid that the Egyptian troops in North Yemen would try to force Britain out of the Middle East. Saudi Arabia and Britain, therefore, gave weapons and money to Badr's supporters.

A BRIEF REPUBLIC

For eight years, civil war raged in North Yemen. By 1967 Egypt had lost twenty thousand soldiers in North Yemen, without stabilizing the country. Frustrated by the lack of success and distracted by problems at home, Egypt withdrew its troops. Most people thought the revolution would fail without Egypt's help, but the YAR forces managed to hold on. Badr's followers laid siege to Sanaa for three months but failed to take the city. By 1970 more than two hundred thousand North Yemenis had died in the struggle, and Badr realized he could never win. The two sides finally agreed to peace, with the republicans in control.

Under the rule of Yahya's son, Ahmad, North Yemen remained poor and underdeveloped.

Peace brought new problems, however. The republicans had agreed that they wanted to eliminate the imam's rule, but they agreed on nothing else. Politicians bickered and failed to provide even basic services to the country. Some tribes withdrew their support from the government. A series of prime ministers ruled for short periods without building a strong government. In the late 1970s, two leaders were assassinated in less than a year.

The situation started to improve after Colonel Ali Abdallah Salih became president of North Yemen in 1978. Salih appointed an advisory council that represented nearly every class and political ideology. The government began providing more services, which meant hiring more employees. With these new job opportunities, the economy improved. The government, however, got nearly half its budget from foreign aid. North Yemen's life expectancy was only about fifty years, and its health care system was the worst in the Middle East, covering only a quarter of the population.

NATIONALISM IN THE SOUTH

Meanwhile, South Yemen had been going through a revolution of its own. In order to keep control of its protectorate, Britain discouraged social, economic, or political development in South Yemen. A huge gap grew between the prosperous few and the desperately poor majority of South Yemenis. Many people resented their lack of opportunities, their country's outdated political and social systems, and the rule by foreigners.

Various rebel groups in South Yemen agitated for independence. The National Liberation Front (NLF), which promoted armed struggle to force Britain out of South Yemen, quickly gained popularity. Author Helen Lackner writes, "The mass of workers in Aden turned towards the NLF as they found the

Members of the National Liberation Front take to the streets of Aden in 1967. The NLF expelled the British from South Yemen.

concept of armed struggle appealing, sometimes on the basis of clearly reasoned political argument but also possibly as a modernised form of traditional tribal armed conflict."[27] The rebels' goals included free education for everyone, equality between men and women, the development of modern agriculture, better health care, and the reunification of North and South Yemen.

In 1966 and 1967 the NLF took over many regions outside Aden. In June 1967 it captured part of Aden for two weeks. Soon it had defeated all rival rebel groups and gained the support of the South Yemeni army. By September, Britain acknowledged that it had lost control of South Yemen. In November Britain withdrew entirely and handed the country over to the NLF. The National Liberation Front declared South Yemen independent and renamed it the People's Republic of South Yemen.

STRUGGLING TO SURVIVE

Even after Britain's withdrawal, conflict continued as South Yemen's leaders fought each other. Two years after independence, the most radical group within the NLF gained power. They envisioned a country built on Communist principles: The government would own all property, religion would have no place in law or government, and no political parties could form besides the Communist Party.

Other Communist countries, such as the Soviet Union and the People's Republic of China, gave money and provided political advisers to the new nation. Despite this help, the radicals failed to build a strong government. As in the North, the government could not control tribal leaders, and politicians fought each other over many issues. Although the government tried to improve health care and education, by 1985 life expectancy was only about fifty years, and just 35 percent of adults could read. More than half the people in South Yemen depended on subsistence agriculture, but farmers suffered from long droughts and occasional floods. The yearly income per person was just a few hundred dollars. Political unrest grew, leading to a civil war in 1986 that damaged housing, businesses, and roads. With few ways to generate income, South Yemen depended on foreign aid, mainly from the Soviet Union, and on money sent home by Yemenis working in other countries.

STRAIN BETWEEN THE YEMENS

Leaders in both North and South Yemen dreamed of uniting their countries, but still they fought. The traditional, religious groups in the North were suspicious of Communist South Yemen's secular government. Meanwhile, South Yemen's leaders encouraged Communist groups in the North to rebel. Tensions flared up regularly and resulted in warfare between North and South in 1971, 1978, and 1982. After each of these conflicts, the leaders of the two sides made peace and talked about unification, but the plans led nowhere.

Then in 1988, North and South Yemen fought again, this time over a border region where both sides were prospecting for oil. The two sides eventually agreed to end the conflict and explore for oil and minerals in that area together. They also announced plans for unification once again.

This time South Yemen, in particular, had a reason to pursue unification seriously. Its biggest source of foreign aid, the Soviet Union, had begun to dissolve and could no longer support South Yemen. The Soviets gradually withdrew their financial support, along with their military, economic, and technological advisers in 1989 and 1990.

South Yemen hoped that unification would solve its financial problems. Joining with North Yemen would reconnect South Yemen to the Muslim world; perhaps this would encourage Arab countries to provide financial aid. South Yemen also hoped to benefit from the North's stronger economy.

To prepare for unification, South Yemen reformed its government in several areas. The South's leaders allowed new political parties to form, and passed new laws to encourage foreign investment. According to political scientist Joseph Kostiner, "These efforts. . . reflected the desire of the leadership to create a politically tolerant and liberal image, so as to prepare the population for its encounter with the other Yemeni society."[28] But for ordinary citizens, the issue was simple. They were poor, and unification seemed to promise them more money and more opportunities.

For its part, North Yemen saw unification as a chance to make peace permanently with its southern neighbor. It would also give North Yemen access to the port of Aden on the Red Sea and a pipeline to take oil exports there. Moreover, a large, peaceful Yemen with potential oil reserves might attract foreign investments, which would bring money into the country.

YEMEN'S GOVERNMENT

The government of Yemen is based on a parliamentary system, where people elect their representatives. Everyone over age eighteen can vote. The Council of Representatives has 301 members who are elected to six-year terms. This council, also called the Parliament, passes laws, allocates money to various public projects, approves international treaties, and plans Yemen's future development.

Yemen also has a president and a cabinet of ministers. The president is elected for a seven-year term and can serve up to two terms. He appoints the vice president and prime minister. He also appoints other ministers, with the advice of the prime minister. The president is commander in chief of the military as well as the political leader of the country.

The courts in Yemen uphold the laws passed by the representatives. The 1994 amendments to the constitution state that Yemen's law will be based primarily on Shariah, or Islamic law. Shariah governs many aspects of life, including prayer, marriage, and diet. Yemen's justice system is separate from its government so that judges can work without interference from politicians. Each district has its own court, and cases can be appealed to a higher court. The Supreme Court in Sanaa is the highest court, with a chief justice and a group of seven judges.

A DIFFICULT HONEYMOON

Despite the optimism on both sides, unification did not come easily. Religious and political differences caused tension between North and South. The 2.5 million South Yemenis were mainly Sunni Muslims who were used to a secular government. Over half of the approximately 10 million North Yemenis were also Sunni, but North Yemen had mostly been ruled by a Zaydi Shiite imam from the sixteenth century until 1962. Even after the republican rebellion, Zaydi tribal politics dominated the government, and official policy was rooted in traditional tribal and Islamic values. Kostiner writes, "The leaders of both states shared the drive towards unity, aiming at the establishment of a strong, economically sound and peaceful unified country. However, there were residual feelings of suspicion and rivalry carried over from the differences and past hostility between the two states."[29]

The leaders who were in favor of unification wanted to act before their opponents could organize resistance. They

Pedestrians walk beneath a large mural of President Salih. Salih was the first president of a unified Yemen.

quickly agreed on some basic principles, and the Republic of Yemen was declared on May 22, 1990. North Yemen's president, Ali Abdallah Salih, became the president of the new nation, while the south provided a vice president, Ali Salim Al-Bidh, and the prime minister, Haidar Abu Bakr al-Attash. Most government posts were divided equally between people from the north and the south. Sanaa became the political capital of Yemen, while Aden became the official economic capital. A new constitution promised people equality, the right to own private property, and a respect of basic human rights. Leaders would eventually be elected by the people, and a variety of political parties could form. Freedom of speech and of the press increased.

In an election held in May 1991, most Yemenis voted in favor of unification. The government's leaders planned to combine the political and economic systems of the two countries within thirty months. President Salih claimed, "The new state has removed forever the imaginary borderlines created during partition and is now embarking on a new era."[30] However, this unity was in name only. Few government agencies had merged or were even working together. Laws had been passed to unify banking, taxation, customs, and other government policies, but in reality north and south continued to work separately. Water, electricity, and telecommunications systems in the two halves were independent of each other.

Politicians from the north and south remained suspicious of each other. They made alliances, but at the same time tried to keep their own power and weaken their old enemies.

The government spent its energy on infighting and did nothing to educate the average Yemeni about the new system.

Although most people liked the idea of unification, they still recalled tribal rivalries and held bitter memories of old fights. Southerners who had gotten used to Communist rule resented a return to tribal politics. Meanwhile, religious leaders in the north were afraid that secular ideas would weaken their people's religious values.

Citizens throughout the country were suspicious of the government and believed that politicians were interested only in money and power. They resented the fact that government officials often lived lavishly while ordinary people were poor. Many people, inside and outside the country, doubted that Yemeni unity would last. By late 1992, writes Dresch, "with the two major parties [i.e., north and south] at odds no decisions were possible and the State seemed to be disintegrating."[31]

An image of President Salih graces the Parliament building in Sanaa.

PEACE AT LAST

The first elections for Parliament were held on April 27, 1993, and members were elected from several different political groups. Conflicts began almost at once, however, as rivals tried to settle old scores. Vice President Al-Bidh left the government. Then in May 1994, the south tried to secede from the union and Yemen exploded in civil war. The north's greater military power allowed it to quickly take control, capturing Aden on July 7. The resistance collapsed, and most southern leaders fled. President Salih offered amnesty to all but a few, so many soon returned to Yemen.

Northern Yemen's victory gave its politicians greater control of the government. They wrote a series of amendments to the constitution that changed the government to more closely follow the north's policies, basing all law on Islamic law.

Yemen had started the twentieth century as two countries ruled by foreign powers, with a medieval, tribal society. Yemen ended that century as a single united country trying hard to modernize its government, economy, and social structure. After the civil war, several international agencies, including the International Monetary Fund and the World Bank, helped Yemen reorganize its economy. The process is ongoing, as Yemen tries to control its spending, reform the civil service, and sell state-owned businesses to private investors. The discovery of new oil fields also helped bring in money, and the government hopes to discover more oil.

When the country is financially stable, job opportunities, health care, and education should all improve for the average Yemeni. These improvements are necessary to create happy citizens and therefore a peaceful country. Some early signs are hopeful. In September 1999, Yemen held its first direct presidential elections. International observers claim that the elections were, for the most part, fair and peaceful. The people reelected President Salih by a large majority. Although Yemen faces many challenges, most Yemenis entered the new millennium with a sense of hope for their future and pride in the land of their ancestors.

Daily Life in Yemen

4

Yemen was largely isolated from the rest of the world until the revolutions of the 1960s. Cut off from political, economic, and social developments, Yemenis lived much as their ancestors had lived. Even today, because Yemen joined the modern world so late, the Yemeni people still follow many ancient traditions in terms of work, marriage, and social life. Much of this heritage comes from Islam. Yemen still largely follows a class system based on Muslim ancestry, and Islam rules many aspects of daily life, such as the roles of men and women.

Parts of Yemen are changing rapidly, however, especially the cities. The 1960s revolutions, and then unification in 1990, brought not only political changes but also new ideas about how people should live. Modern society is breaking down class barriers, and people in Yemen today have more choices about their education and work. Still, tradition plays a large role in everyday life. Most Yemenis want to hold on to Islam and their Yemeni heritage as they join the modern world.

The Prophet's Descendants

In traditional Yemeni society, every person was born into a rigid social caste system. Caste was largely determined by how closely one was related to the Prophet Muhammad. Children belonged to their father's caste, and this determined whether they became teachers, farmers, or laborers. Women could marry men of their own caste or a higher one, but not lower. This caste system is still in place, though in modern Yemen there is greater social mobility than in the past.

At the top of Yemeni society are the *sayyids*, who are said to be direct descendants of the Prophet Muhammad. In the past, they traditionally had more power, education, and wealth than other Yemenis. They were the judges, religious teachers, healers, and political leaders. The imams who ruled Yemen were always *sayyids*. Since the revolutions, the power and status of *sayyids* has diminished. Although they are still often wealthy and well educated, they are less likely to follow

Yemen's sayyids *live in opulent homes like this. Modern Yemen is beginning to dissolve traditional class distinctions.*

their traditional roles. Many are still teachers and administrators, but some have traded prestige for financial opportunity and taken on lower-status jobs as merchants.

One level below *sayyids* are the *qadis;* in the past, they were an educated elite, despite not being descendants of the Prophet. In most of the Muslim world, a *qadi* is a judge of Islamic law, but in Yemen today they may also be teachers or administrators.

The *qabayl* are rural tribespeople, and were generally farmers. The *qabayl* traditionally protected the *sayyids*, *qadis*, and lower-class people associated with their tribes. Many *qabayl* are still farmers, but some now move to cities or to foreign countries to find work.

DESCENDANTS OF NO ONE
The lowest class in Yemeni society includes several groups, such as the *bani khums* and *akhdem*, who have no important ancestors or whose ancestry is unknown. This class traditionally performed despised work, which in Yemen included jobs such as barber, bathkeeper, butcher, innkeeper, and

musician. They received food or money from the tribes as payment. In the past, they did not farm, though some have now bought land. Another low-status group, the *abid*, was descended from slaves brought from Africa. Until the abolition of slavery, the *abid* were used as farm labor in the Tihama. Many *abid* are still farmers, but now they have the freedom to own land or to seek other jobs.

In the past, status was evident by people's clothes, the type of dagger worn by men, the dances people did, and even the foods they ate. In recent years, the caste system has lessened as more people move to the cities, adopt Western dress, and eat imported foods.

In modern Yemen the importance and rigidity of social status varies between regions. In some cases people may be able to rise in social rank through education. In addition, Yemenis who worked abroad and came home rich have in some areas created new classes based on wealth rather than birth. The U.S. government publication *The Yemens: Country Studies* reported that, by 1985, "many North Yemenis wished to deny the importance of traditional status groups, but most continued to contract marriages along status lines, and nowhere were despised occupations performed by any but members of the lowest-status groups."[32] The caste system is less important in southern Yemen, where the socialist leadership tried to wipe out class distinctions following the revolution in 1967.

URBAN MEN AND FARMERS

Despite the expansion of job opportunities since unification, most people follow traditional roles and are farmers like their ancestors. Today some 60 percent of the Yemeni people still work in agriculture, but earning a living by farming is a struggle. Farms are usually small and produce barely enough to feed the farmer's family, with little left over to sell. In a bad year, droughts, floods, or windstorms can destroy crops. Few rural homes have electricity or gas, so they must use charcoal or wood for heating and cooking. Farmers often can barely afford the basic necessities, and have little hope of making enough money to afford simple luxuries. Paul Dresch notes, "The dream of independent people to live off their own land is now as difficult to realise in Yemen as it is anywhere—food, clothes, machinery all require money."[33]

Young people who want a better future are moving to the cities to look for work, but jobs are hard to find. Some people work in the oil fields or in construction. The service sector provides jobs in fields such as shipping, insurance, and tourism, and there are also some government jobs. A few jobs are available in factories, which produce mostly packaged foods, cigarettes, and household products. Many men continue to seek work abroad. More than four hundred thousand Yemenis are working in Saudi Arabia, with smaller numbers in other countries. Though some settle abroad permanently, most work for just a few years to save money for their return. Those working abroad also often send money home to their family members.

Because Yemeni families are typically large, each worker supports on average four to five other people. According to *The Yemens: Country Studies*, "The decision for a man to migrate was seldom made by individual choice; the entire extended family participated in the decision and benefited from remittances [money sent home]."[34] When migrants return home, they often spend their extra money on land, building a home, starting a business, buying a taxi or truck, or paying for a marriage.

WOMEN

When men leave their villages for jobs in the cities or in foreign countries, the women they leave behind must take on extra farm duties. This migration of men off the farms means that Yemeni women perform an estimated 70 to 75 percent of all agricultural work. They herd cattle, spread manure in the fields, plow, sow seeds, harvest, and thresh the grain. In addition, women have always been responsible for looking after the home—caring for the children, collecting firewood, fetching water, and cooking, often over a smoky wood stove. Water is not easily available in much of the country, so women must often walk long distances to reach a well. In the highlands, many women balance heavy containers on their heads as they hike steep mountain paths to fetch water or wood.

Sometimes men working abroad send home money so that women can purchase appliances to make their work easier. Women do not, however, gain authority in the absence of their husbands. As explained in *The Yemens*, "Men tended to send remittances home to male relatives rather

SHOPPING IN YEMEN

In *Arabia Felix*, Pascal Maréchaux describes the market in the mountain village of Tur:

> Each street of the *souk* [market] has its own speciality: hats, pottery, sandals, cloth, herbs and medicinal powders, all laid out in profusion; baskets made of the hide of cows and dromedaries [camels]....Business is conducted in an undertone. An old man strokes his beard, his questioner takes out a few banknotes, which are refused, and the bargaining goes on. The fat of the sheep's rump must be felt, the cow prodded and poked, the dromedary's teeth inspected.

In contrast, in urban Sanaa,

> For good or ill, the *souk* has succumbed to the brash charms of modern life. Radios are decorated with baubles and gold braid, cars are upholstered in fake fur, shops decked with trash, and the taxis flaunt brightly coloured electric light bulbs on top of their radio aerials—which must be a good six feet long. Workmen...fabricate buckets and shoes out of old car tyres. The blacksmiths use scrap from old cars.

A butcher displays meat in an open-air market.

than to wives. Even when money was sent to wives, the husband's male relative whom he had appointed guardian of his wife in his absence made the major decisions as to how the money would be spent."[35]

Initially, the constitution of unified Yemen promised women equal rights. After the civil war in 1994, however, the constitution was changed to follow northern Yemen's Islamic practices more closely, stating that wives must obey their husbands. Some women today are fighting for more rights, and President Salih is considered an advocate of women's rights. Women can vote and generally have better opportunities for education and employment than they had in the past. Scholar Tim Mackintosh-Smith points out that, "at least in Yemen, in contrast to [places like] Saudi Arabia, women are able to drive cars, enter Parliament, [and] become top-ranking civil servants."[36]

Urban women often face discrimination in the workplace, but, in the city of Taiz, where women merchants work in the

Women offer fruit for sale in a crowded Taiz market. Women across Yemen are starting to work outside of the home.

markets, and have done so for years. The women there are famous for both their beauty and their tough bargaining. According to author Pertti Hamalainen,

> There are many stories about how this came about. The
> most popular tells that the men used to do the selling
> here just like everywhere in Yemen. In the evenings,
> however, they were so exhausted by the arduous climb
> back to the mountain that they neglected their wives at
> home. The unsatisfied women turned to the imam for
> advice. The imam, to demonstrate how overburdened
> their husbands were, suggested the women do the sell-
> ing instead. They took up the challenge and have, ever
> since, dominated the market.[37]

In other cities, more women are starting to work outside the
home. Women who study at a university can choose from
programs in education, business, medicine, science, law, or
the arts. They are especially sought after as teachers.

A BRIEF CHILDHOOD

The average Yemeni woman's primary duty, however, remains taking care of her family. Yemeni families are large, as
women have an average of seven babies. Children look after
younger siblings and help their parents in the house or on
the farm. Pascal Maréchaux writes,

> [Children] play their part in all the daily tasks, the girls
> stay at their mother's side, helping in the kitchen and
> in the fields, and the boys accompany their fathers
> everywhere….They take on responsibilities in child-
> hood, and when they cease to be children they become
> adults. Adolescence is a meaningless concept here.
> Once a boy is circumcised he is given his *djambia* [dag-
> ger], a young girl is given her veil, and with them they
> acquire a clearly defined status in society.[38]

Besides learning traditional skills, many children now go
to school. In the past, most children studied at the village
mosque, where they learned to memorize the Koran. Few
even learned to read or write. When the two Yemens united,
however, the constitution gave everyone the right to an education. Now the government requires all children to attend
school from ages six to fifteen. Schoolchildren learn to read

and write Arabic, and English is often taught as a foreign language. Some children go on to secondary schools until age eighteen.

Though education is required by law, not all children are able to go to school. Some small villages do not have schools. And even when there is a school nearby, some families cannot afford to send their children. School itself is free, but parents still have to pay for books, supplies, and clothing, which can make school too expensive for many families. Today some people are choosing to have smaller families so that they can afford to educate their children, in the hope that schooling will lead to better lives.

Many parents, however, do not see the value of educating their children, especially the girls. Over 90 percent of six-year-old boys start school, but less than half of six-year-old girls do. In 1992, a quarter of the students in grades one through six were girls, while only 14 percent in grades seven through twelve were girls. Not only do some parents see no need for girls to receive an education, but some, adhering to strict Islamic beliefs, do not want their daughters associating with male teachers. In some urban areas girls make up about half the student body in the early grades, but rural girls are especially unlikely to go to school. In remote areas the school may be far away, and while many parents allow boys to walk to school alone, they will not allow girls to do so. Some girls are forced to stay home for lack of an escort.

Current numbers are lacking, but in 1992, less than one-fifth of children ages five to nineteen attended school. In part, this is simply a result of economics. Yemen suffers from a shortage of laborers because many adult men emigrate to foreign countries to work. So, businesses and even government agencies are forced to hire teenagers and even pre-teens. Other children work in family businesses, helping out at their parents' store or restaurant. Because so many children enter the workforce, Yemen has trouble improving the level of education in its population.

DIVISION OF THE SEXES

Except for siblings, boys and girls in Yemen are generally kept separate, following Muslim tradition. As in most Islamic countries, modesty is valued and women rarely associate with men other than family members. Even in a small village,

THE STATUS OF WOMEN

After the 1960s revolutions, modernization brought changes to Yemeni society, especially regarding the role of women. In North Yemen, women started working in factories, schools, banks, businesses, and even government ministries. Socialist South Yemen tried to change the status of women even more. The government started literacy campaigns aimed at women, opened all schools to women, encouraged the employment of women, and established some child care centers. A family law passed there in 1974 prohibited arranged marriages, restricted the ability of a man to marry more than one wife, and gave women and men equal rights in divorce.

The effect was mixed. Many people saw little reason for women to learn to read, but nevertheless some women took advantage of their new opportunities. By 1984 half of South Yemen's medical school graduates were women. Today, in unified Yemen, women make up about 20 percent of the paid workforce. Although a few women hold jobs in nearly every field, more than 80 percent of working women work in farming or fishing, compared with about 35 percent of men who work in these fields. Other common paid jobs for women include factory work, mining, clerical work, health care, handicrafts such as sewing, and teaching. Far more women work without pay, however, mostly on family farms.

Officially, Yemen's constitution gives women the same general rights as men. However, specific laws discriminate against women. Men can divorce at will, but women must sue for divorce. Divorced mothers lose custody of their children if they remarry; fathers do not. Daughters inherit half as much as sons, and if a woman is murdered, her family receives in compensation half of what a murdered man's family would receive. Women are also not allowed to testify in criminal cases. Women who are imprisoned are only released into the custody of a male guardian, though no law actually requires this. If no guardian claims them, women prisoners are kept beyond the end of their sentence.

Only about 6 percent of Yemeni women vote, whereas 94 percent of men do. Though women can hold political office, very few do. Two women were elected in 1993, but a few years later Parliament was totally male. Only about a quarter of the registered voters are women, but that number has been increasing.

A young man arranges a display of daggers in a bazaar. Most Yemeni children must work, and few are able to attend school.

boys and girls may know each other by sight, but have never had a chance for a long conversation.

Because young men and women have few ways to meet potential spouses, parents often arrange marriages for their children. A mother will look for a suitable bride for her son. If her husband and son agree with her choice, they will talk to the girl's family. The girl's parents consult with her. In theory, a couple must agree to their marriage, but that does not always happen, according to *The Yemens: Country Studies:* "Marriages are arranged between families, and the bride and groom often have little say in their nuptials."[39] Once a marriage has been agreed upon, the families set a date for a formal betrothal. This is a simple ceremony in which the groom's family delivers gifts to the bride's house. Then they choose a date for the wedding.

The wedding ceremony often takes several days. Typically, neighborhood women climb onto the roof of the house and welcome the couple with singing. The groom arrives with a group of singing and dancing men. The bride comes later with her father. Everyone feasts, though the men and women often eat separately. Author Eric Hansen describes the men at one wedding feast: "Yemenis eat quickly, and soon the long table-tops were ravaged as a result of the feasting. There were the usual joints of stewed mutton and a fatty soup of bone marrow and goat vertebrae....Soon it was time for the platters of stewed sheep's heads....The tabletops and carpeted floor of the dining room were littered with glistening jawbones and broken skulls."[40]

Yemen has no minimum legal age for marriage, and girls may marry as young as age nine. Most girls, however, marry between the ages of sixteen and eighteen, and nearly all women are married by age twenty-five. Their husbands are usually six to eight years older. Islam allows men to have up to four wives, as long as each wife is treated equally. However, in Yemen, few men can afford to support more than one wife. Only about 7 percent of married women share their husband with another wife.

MARRIAGE AND MONEY

Marriage in Yemen often comes down to money. Men essentially buy a wife by paying a bride-price to the bride's

Veiled Yemeni women pose with children for a photo. Women face a great deal of discrimination in Yemen.

family. The amount expected for a bride-price rose dramatically in the 1970s and 1980s as a result of men working abroad. *The Yemens: Country Studies* explains: "Migrants could afford to pay more for a wife so that the cost of marriage for all grooms increased, and many prospective grooms were forced to migrate to Saudi Arabia to work in order to pay for marriage costs."[41]

In 1990 the average price for a Yemeni bride was $2,000 to $4,000. Most of the money goes to the bride's family. The bride herself keeps between 10 percent and half, depending on local custom. The bride's share of the bride-price belongs entirely to her after marriage, even in the case of a divorce.

Divorce is fairly common in Yemen. In some areas up to 20 percent of women may divorce at some point in their lives. Unlike in most other Arab countries, divorce does not destroy a woman's future, and she will likely remarry. Until then, divorced women usually move back in with their parents.

Widows also tend to live with their parents, or their children. In fact, few Yemenis live alone, and often many generations live in one house. According to Pertti Hamalainen, "Usually, each Yemeni house is inhabited by several generations of the same extended family. . . a man, his wives, his sons and unmarried daughters, and his sons' wives and children."[42]

SOCIAL GATHERINGS

Big families may live in one house, but the men and women lead largely separate lives. Most social occasions are segregated by gender. At least once a week, and in some cases every day, men spend the afternoon at a party where they chew the leaves of the shrub *qat*. They gather in the top floor of the house, known as the *mafraj*. Michael Jenner describes the *mafraj*:

> Its four sides are lined with mattresses and cushions; the middle of the room is left open....It is essentially a male preserve used for receiving visitors, relaxing, chatting, eating, and chewing the narcotic leaves of *qat*. It is a fact that most important matters in Yemen are discussed and resolved during lengthy afternoon *qat* sessions, so the *mafraj* functions equally as council chamber and living room.[43]

Chewing *qat* makes people energetic for a few hours, after which they become quiet and perhaps melancholy. *The Yemens: Country Studies* describes a typical party: "After the drug takes effect men talk animatedly, and many local political decisions are made in qat sessions. Men hold intimate talks or philosophical discussions and on occasion may dance with the *jambiyyas* [daggers]. The guests' liveliness is succeeded by silence or quiet conversation, and they eventually depart quietly."[44]

While the men are chewing *qat*, women are also socializing in their friends' homes. Urban women often drink tea and soft drinks at these gatherings, and they frequently perform traditional Yemeni dances. Some may chew *qat*, while others prefer snacks such as nuts or raisins. Rural women rarely chew *qat*, because many think the drug weakens the body and makes working more difficult.

FESTIVE FOOD

Though food is not a major feature of most *qat* parties, it is an important part of hospitality in Yemen. Hansen explains, "The refusal to take food in Yemen, as in other Arabic and Asian countries, can mean one of only three things: that the guest feels the host cannot afford to provide food, which shames him; that the food is unclean or not well prepared; or that the guest has such a hatred for the host that he does not wish to diminish that hatred by sharing food. To refuse hospitality can be a serious matter."[45]

Each region and tribe has its own special dishes, but throughout Yemen women prepare simple dishes using grains, vegetables, and fruits. In the coastal areas, fish is also common. Meat, eggs, and milk are expensive, so most people save them for special occasions. Few Muslims ever eat pork or drink alcohol, because those items are forbidden by Islam.

A festive meal may start with *bint al-sahn*, a round egg bread sprinkled with blackened seeds and drenched in honey and butter. For special occasions, cooks may serve a whole sheep, stuffed with rice, hard-boiled eggs, and raisins. Other popular dishes include *saltah*, a spicy stew of meat and beans; *hilbah*, a tangy dip with tomato and garlic, served with bread; and *shafout*, yogurt flavored with garlic, chilies, and cilantro, which is eaten as soup or served over platter-size pancakes.

A father holds some qat *before his son's nose. The narcotic plays an important part in male social interaction.*

For most meals, people sit on the floor and take food from communal dishes. They do not use forks but, instead, scoop up food with a piece of bread or their right hand. Lunch is the biggest meal of the day and may involve several courses, including a dessert of fruit or pudding. Yemenis often end a meal with strong, sweet tea. *Qishr*, another popular drink, is made from ground coffee bean husks and ginger; it is cheaper than drinking real coffee.

Yemeni cooks often prepare these foods in the same way their ancestors did. The traditional Yemeni kitchen has a cylindrical clay oven that is heated with a charcoal or wood fire. Flat bread is slapped onto the inside wall of the oven to bake. Other food is cooked on a grill set over the top opening. In villages that do not have electricity, people keep food cool not in refrigerators but in a special cupboard in the wall. Wind blows through holes in the outside wall and around a big jar of water, which evaporates and keeps the food cool. Urban homes often have a gas stove and electric refrigerator, but cooks still prepare many of the same foods as their rural counterparts.

Most Yemenis treasure their traditional foods and customs. Yet life is changing as modern conveniences make their way even to remote areas. People are more likely to have radios, trucks, and perhaps diesel generators to pump water. In the cities especially, the outside world has greatly influenced daily living. Urban Yemenis may wear European clothes, eat imported foods, use electrical appliances, and watch television. People throughout the country now have better opportunities for education and jobs, and more choices about how to live their lives. In the last few years, Yemen has entered the modern world. But heritage and tradition remain important forces in Yemen. They influence many aspects of daily life, from social customs and cuisine to the arts.

5

THE ARTS OF YEMEN

The majority of Yemenis live in the foothills and mountains, in villages that until recently were isolated from the outside world. The rugged terrain even tended to isolate one village from another. Villagers seldom visited other villages since travel was so difficult. Because villagers rarely interacted with outsiders, over time they developed unique styles of housing, clothing, music, and dance.

Though specific details of culture vary throughout Yemen, they are connected by the influence of Islam. What sets Islam apart from most religions and makes its influence distinctive is a long tradition of not depicting humans or animals in works of art. Interestingly, this tradition is not based in scripture. According to the book *Aramco and Its World*, "The Quran [Koran] nowhere prohibits the representation of humans or animals in drawings or paintings, but as Islam expanded in its early years it inherited some of the prejudices against visual art of this kind that had already taken root in the Middle East.... Islamic law banned the use of images and declared that the painter of animate figures would be damned on the Day of Judgement."[46] Islamic judges decided that since God is the only being able to create life, artists should not try to imitate God by painting or sculpting living creatures. Instead, works of art influenced by Islam often feature geometric designs, floral patterns, and Arabic calligraphy, or decorative writing.

Despite Islamic traditions, in modern times Yemenis have gotten used to seeing images of people on television and in newspapers. Photos of political leaders are often displayed in homes and businesses. Display of these images has encouraged a new willingness to create art that shows living things.

ARABIC LANGUAGE AND LITERATURE
Yemeni artistic traditions also show the broad influence of Arabic language and culture. Arabic is known for its beauty, in both written and spoken form. Many Arabs love musical

sounds, emotional words, exaggeration, and symbolism. Poetry and even speeches may be composed more for the way the words sound than for their meaning. As a result, Yemen has a long tradition of oral literature.

In the past, stories were often passed down orally in Yemen, since few people could read or write. Professional storytellers repeated popular tales, perhaps adding new twists to keep the audience entertained. These stories were often based on the exploits of real people, such as tribal or national heroes.

The earliest written works were typically fables, anecdotes, or works of history or science. The Yemeni author best known outside of Yemen may be a historian from the tenth century named Al-Hamdani. He traveled widely and recorded what he learned about southern Arabian history from previous centuries. Al-Hamdani's works are notable for their accuracy—archaeologists still use his texts to help find the lost ruins of ancient kingdoms.

Women in traditional costumes herd their goats. Most Yemenis live in isolated villages.

CALLIGRAPHY

Books may be appreciated for the information they contain, but they may also be works of art. Arabic script is famous for its beauty, and the proper calligraphy style can add to the meaning and emotion of the words. A skilled calligrapher can write Arabic in many different styles, to create different moods. Some calligraphy scripts are heavy and angular, while others are rounded and flowing or bold and sweeping. In one variation, the text is worked into a pattern in which the two halves form a mirror image. For pictorial calligraphy, a passage is written in the shape of an object, perhaps a mosque or a tree.

Calligraphy may be used to decorate buildings, particularly mosques. Passages from the Koran, painted on tiles or carved into stone, often decorate the walls of mosques. The words, written with beautiful grace, are meant to inspire spirituality. There are over forty thousand mosques in Yemen, some of them lovely works of art with ornate decorations. Today Islamic calligraphers continue to develop new styles and to create works of art with the written word.

Intricate calligraphy borders this sixteenth-century illustration of Noah and his ark.

As literacy has increased in recent decades, written fiction has grown popular in Yemen. Modern novels tend to explore themes that are Yemeni in nature, such as the strain of living under oppression or the loneliness of emigration. Few of these books are known outside the country, and few have been translated into English. One exception is *The Hostage*, by Zayd Muti Dammaj, Yemen's foremost novelist. The novel, set in North Yemen before the revolution, is about a boy taken hostage by the imam in order to ensure his father's political loyalty. While working as a servant, the boy observes the ancient social order and corruption of the palace.

POLITICAL POETRY

Like stories, poems were traditionally memorized and passed down orally. The *qasidah*, a long poem that tells of a hero's journey through many dangers, is one popular art form. Other memorized poems may honor a dead hero or praise a generous person. Love poems are also favorites, and religious poetry may use similar language to express a love for God.

In the past, Yemeni poems always followed very strict rhyming patterns. Today, however, traditional poetry has been joined by newer styles, such as unrhymed free verse. Many poems are short, perhaps only two lines, but some have up to two hundred verses.

Tribal tradition holds that everyone should be able to compose poetry, and doing so is a popular form of entertainment in Yemen. At many social events, the men challenge each other to a poetry competition to show off their wit. Guests insult each other in rhyme, then apologize, still using poetry. At other times, two poets will take turns making up verses of a poem. During weddings, guests often work together to create a spontaneous poem as a gift to the bride and groom.

Yemeni poetry is popular entertainment, but it can also be a form of social or political activism. People use poetry to debate issues at every level, from the family to international politics. For example, a young woman may compose and recite a poem to let her parents know how she feels about their choice of a husband for her. In the political arena, a poet can influence and motivate many people. During the northern civil war, for example, the politician and poet Mohammed al

Zubayri used poetry to inspire the republicans in their fight against the royalists. Meanwhile, the royalists expressed their feelings in poems such as this one:

> The high cliffs called and every notable in Yemen answered:
> We'll never go republican, not if we are wiped off the earth,
> Not if yesterday returns today and the sun rises in Aden,
> Not if the earth catches fire and the sky rains lead.[47]

After the revolutions, people used poetry to express their political opinions and their hopes for the future. Today many political poems are distributed on cassette tapes. Ordinary citizens record poems that are critical of the government, while the government hires its own poets to record replies.

Even warring tribes negotiate through poetry. In an interview with the *Harvard University Gazette*, Steven C. Caton, professor of contemporary Arab studies at Harvard University, described tribesmen meeting for a negotiation: "As they arrived, they would be chanting poetry. One side would be chanting a poem, and the other side would be listening to it and then would reply. And then the other side, hearing the reply, would chant yet another reply....And they'd often leave chanting poetry, framing their moral positions once again."[48]

In another interview, in *Humanities* magazine, Caton notes, "In places like Yemen, there is a cultural conviction that poetry has something to offer politics—that political action is not only about using brute force, it's about persuading someone, convincing them that what you say is moral and just. They are persuaded in part by the beauty of the language to think so."[49]

THE RHYTHM OF LIFE

Like poetry, music has often been used to discuss politics and encourage change in Yemen. Military songs were especially popular during the 1960s revolutions. In an interview in the *Yemen Times*, singer Iskander Thabet claimed that songs such as "Oh Tyrant, Why All This Oppression" inspired rebellion: "I presented many other songs which psyched up the public and fighters and gave them a moral boost. I think that my songs, as well as those of others, have played a crucial role in rallying the people around the cause of the nation."[50]

Although political songs are common throughout the country, musical styles vary greatly by region. One of the most popular instruments in the mountains is the oud, a lute that looks something like a guitar. In Sanaa, dignified songs are played on an oud, accompanied by a single vocalist. Drums, beaten with the hands, are also common in the highlands. Tihama music features feverish rhythms played on violins, cymbals, and the *simsimiya*, a lyre with five strings. Throughout the country, Yemenis also make music on various types of reed pipes.

One still-popular musical tradition is the work song, although this is declining as the country modernizes. According to A.D. Bakewell of the British-Yemeni Society, "Work songs make up the traditional daily life of both women and

Women perform a traditional dance as part of a celebration. Music and dance play important roles in the daily life of Yemen.

men and, in this category, we can still hear smithy songs, winnowing and grinding songs, songs for drawing water from the well, camel songs and sea shanties. One cannot, however, realistically sing a work song while operating a diesel pump and inevitably they are diminishing with increased mechanisation."[51]

Stereos, radio, and television have also influenced music by spreading regional and foreign songs throughout the country. Music blares through city streets, as taxis and buses play cassettes or the radio at full volume. Besides local poetry chants, love songs, and religious songs, Yemenis enjoy music from Egypt, Lebanon, and the Sudan. Some modern Yemeni music focuses more on the beat than on meaning. Singer Iskander Thabet believes that something is lost in the process: "The new songs focus on the rhythms that make for physical action or movement, which they call dancing. The beauty of the words, the metaphor, the lyric, the dreams, the longings, etc., are lost. All you have is drum-beat that triggers body movement. Often the words are very cheap."[52]

THE JOY OF DANCING

Music often inspires dancing, and Yemenis enjoy many forms of dance. Because the Tihama is so close to Africa, African rhythms have influenced dance in that part of Yemen. Tihama dancing can also involve acrobatics and ceremonial trance. Other regions have their own variations of common dances. One popular dance is the *lu'b*, which is usually performed by pairs of dancers to the accompaniment of love songs or religious hymns. In public the pairs are friends or relatives of the same sex. In most parts of Yemen, men and women dance together only in the privacy of their homes.

Groups of Yemeni women often dance together when they gather for a party. If they do not have musicians among them, they play recorded music. Depending on the music, they may dance alone, in pairs, or in groups to entertain the other female guests. Dance styles vary greatly. Some dances use simple footwork, others are more complex, and one dance uses only hip and torso movements while the feet stay still. Some young women today even dance in modern styles to Western pop music.

Men's dances are often theatrical. They act out war, express the hardship of life, compare two tribes in some way, or express religious beliefs. Some dances are performed for specific occasions, such as a visit to the tomb of an important religious figure.

The *bara'* is a popular men's dance that involves "cutting the air" with daggers. Each tribe has its own version of the *bara'*, performed to different music and with differing dance steps. Men perform the dance outdoors for holidays, to welcome visitors, or just for fun. The dance starts slowly, with the men arranged in a horseshoe shape around a lead dancer. As the pace builds, the men whirl and stomp and slice the air with their daggers. According to guidebook author Hamalainen, "It is a dignified form of art, characterised by patterns of steps, turns, knee bends, hops and jumps, performed publicly in a group, each dancer carrying a dagger, stick or gun....Bara' actually serves to emphasise the cohesion of the group, and it has nothing to do with the frivolity often connected to other types of dance."[53]

JEWELED WEAPONS

The daggers used in the *bara'* are carried by almost every man in Yemen and can be works of art in themselves. *The Yemens: Country Studies* reports that "Traditionally, the kind of *jambiyya*, its sheath, kind of belt, and the position in which it was worn denoted the caste, geographical origin, and tribe of the wearer. By the mid-1980s observers reported that this specificity of *jambiyya* wear was declining, although the popularity of wearing the *jambiyya* remained unabated."[54]

Great care is taken in dagger design. The scabbard may be of carved wood or covered with embroidered cloth, but the handle is the true work of art. Handles may be decorated with silver or studded with coins. The most valuable hilts are made of African rhino horn. These beautiful daggers are tucked into belts of fine cloth or of leather studded with colorful stones. Men may also attach an amulet holder to their belt; these small, decorative silver boxes often hold a slip of paper bearing a verse from the Koran.

Yemeni daggers are mainly ceremonial. Though they are seldom used for practical purposes, they are worn with pride and passed down through the generations. No Yemeni tribesman would leave home without his *jambiyya* in his belt. In recent decades, tribesmen also began carrying rifles and wearing ammunition belts, which might also be lavishly decorated. This public display of weapons reflects the warrior culture that is still strong in Yemen.

Though Yemeni women are unlikely to carry daggers, they too love personal adornment—in the form of jewelry. Markets sell necklaces, heavy bracelets and anklets, earrings, nose rings, amulets, pendant containers for carrying verses from the Koran, and jewelry worn across the forehead like a veil. Most traditional jewelry is made from silver, but necklaces may include coral, amber, or red or black stones. Gold is also becoming more popular as a sign of wealth. For both men and women in Yemen, personal adornment is a way to express their love of decoration.

COLORFUL CLOTHES

Yemeni men typically wear a *futa*, a cloth wrapped around the waist that hangs to just below the knees. Above that they usually wear a shirt and jacket in a style similar to those worn in the West. Most men cover their heads with a white turban or a tall straw hat. In cities men have begun adopting more Western styles, such as suits.

Many Yemenis, both men and women, wear bright colors. Kevin Rushby, in *Eating the Flowers of Paradise*, describes the appearance of men in Taiz: "Silky irridescent greens and mustard, swirling patterns of cinnabar and mauve, purple pom-poms with snazzy belts—the young men wear their futas with...panache."

Women's clothing varies by region. In the Tihama, women wear long colorful dresses, similar to their African neighbors. These dresses are light and loose so that they are cool in the heat of summer. In some mountain towns, women wear bright, embroidered calf-length dresses over snug pants. They wrap long strips of colored cloth around their heads in turbans but often do not veil. In Sanaa, most women wear cloaks that drape from head to foot. They cover their faces with a veil, perhaps a long strip of tie-dyed cloth. For shoes they may wear anything from plastic sandals to pumps. For special occasions, women everywhere drape themselves with silver jewelry.

In some cities, women wear full-body coverings in plain black, a conservative Muslim fashion adopted from Egypt. Yemeni law does not require women to veil. However, many do so because of tradition or a belief that good Muslim women should veil themselves. Other Yemeni women, especially those who are young and educated, cover their heads but not their faces. Some do not even wear a head scarf.

THE BEAUTY OF BUILDINGS

In contrast to the lavish way Yemenis may adorn themselves, their homes are often simple, at least on the outside. Architectural styles vary throughout Yemen and are dictated by the available building materials. In mainland mountain villages, houses often rise six to seven stories high, with stables and storage on the lower levels. The higher floors are the family's living quarters, with bedrooms, kitchens, bathrooms, and a large room for celebrations. The ground floor is usually windowless for privacy, but the top story offers a panoramic view from windows on all sides. Colored glass windows may fill the room with jeweled light.

Pascal Maréchaux described a visit to the village of Beit Idhaqa in the western highlands: "In the sticky midday heat, I climb to the village perched high on the ridge. Set there on the rocky crag it merges with its surroundings, making it hard to separate the natural from the man-made world. The houses are built close together, forming a solid wall. Their windows are edged with white: bold and imaginative patterns that stand out in the distance, designed apparently to attract the light and keep away the flies."[55]

Homes in the Hadramawt villages are made of mud brick and clustered together for security. In the Hadramawt town of Shibam, about seven thousand people live in some five hundred skyscrapers packed close together. The tall buildings look like modern apartments, but these homes may be over five hundred years old and are made of mud. Even tall mosque towers, hotels, palaces, and airports use mud bricks on a stone foundation, though whitewash and paint may disguise the mud.

In contrast, homes in the Tihama are spread out more. A family often has several one-room huts; they might sleep in one, cook in another, and entertain in a third. Sometimes they build walls of stone or earth around their cluster of huts. Maréchaux described the Tihama village of Qanawis: "In the sun-soaked plain, a few palm trees and some fields signal the proximity of the next village: straw huts with conical roofs cluster together inside palisades of thorn bushes and plaited rope.... The roofs are held in place by a fine net of plaited straw, and on the inside are caked with mud, on which the women paint simple geometrical and figurative designs, and fashion shelves to hold their prized enamelled plates."[56]

VISUAL ARTS

In the Arab world, art was traditionally decorative and appeared on useful objects, such as buildings, blankets, or books. Individual works of art that existed for their own sake, such as paintings and sculptures with no practical use, were unknown. Today, however, some artists in Yemen are producing paintings that stand alone. They are also putting aside the traditional Islamic prohibition of representing people. Many of today's artists capture the world around them through portraits or street scenes. Karen Dabrowska, reporting on an exhibit of Yemeni art that toured Britain, noted that "the artists are drawn to the scenery, landscape and self assured figures in traditional dress, proud of their heritage and culture."[57]

This kind of art, although relatively new to Yemen, has found support there. The first art gallery in Yemen opened in 1984 in Aden. Two years later, one of Yemen's most popular artists, Fuad al-Futaih, opened Gallery Number One in Sanaa. This gallery displays work by both Yemeni and foreign artists. Al-Futaih also directs the National Art Center, which exhibits works by artists from Yemen and other countries.

Artists also benefit from the Yemen International Cultural Circle, an organization that promotes the visual arts in Yemen. This group tries to expose Yemeni artists to new techniques and styles, while publicizing the work of Yemen's contemporary artists. Though most Yemeni artists now paint landscapes or people in a representational fashion, some explore modern art with abstract forms or mixed media.

One of Yemen's most famous artists is the painter Amnah Al Nassiri. She often uses modern artistic techniques to explore contemporary social issues. As Yemen's only art critic, Al Nassiri tries to promote modern art in general and the work of women artists in particular. In a *Yemen Times* interview, she said, "Some of the obstacles facing women preventing them from nourishing their talents, in general, are social constraints, economic problems, the way the Yemeni society views women, and the like. I wish the Yemeni female painters to go out of their self exile."[58] With women like Al Nassiri leading the way, the role of women in the arts is changing, along with so much else in Yemen.

Islam and ancient Yemeni traditions still dominate the arts, but as Yemen enters the modern world, the people are

TOYS AND GAMES

Like children everywhere, Yemeni children love games. Soccer is the most popular team sport. Children also play cards, marbles, dominoes, and board games such as backgammon. Girls may play with dolls, while children of both genders sing, dance, and make up poetry.

Most Yemeni children are not able to buy toys, so they make their own from whatever materials are at hand. In *Motoring with Mohammed*, Eric Hansen describes two Yemeni boys playing darts: "The boys had made their darts from discarded syringes. Chicken feathers were attached to the plungers to improve the balance and flight, and the darts thudded into a piece of white Styrofoam with surprising accuracy." "Another boy," Hansen adds, "had made a windmill-like propeller from the split neck of a plastic water bottle. As he ran or faced the wind, it spun rapidly in front of his face. …With head down and arms held out like airplane wings, the boy shuffled his bare feet excitedly and then blasted off."

Yemeni children, like these two young girls, must make their own toys.

Two women chat in a market in the city of Sanaa. Many rural Yemenis are moving to the cities.

exposed to more outside influences. Television, radio, and foreign visitors bring new ideas and styles into the country. Rural Yemenis are moving away from their home villages and mingling in larger cities. New goods made from plastic, metal, or imported cloth are now available in Yemen. People no longer need to weave clothes from cotton, blankets from wool, or baskets and hats from palm fronds. This makes life easier, but one consequence of such modernization is the loss of ancient local traditions.

Yet some modern developments can also help preserve Yemen's heritage. Traditional poems and songs are now recorded onto tapes or broadcast over the radio. Stories and poems that were previously only recited orally are also being written down, so they will not be forgotten. Yemeni painters capture the world around them in bright landscapes or portraits, recording scenes or styles of dress that may someday disappear. As the outside world increasingly influences Yemen's society, the arts provide a link to the country's history and tradition.

6 MODERN CHALLENGES

A Yemeni in traditional dress browses the Internet. Moving into the twenty-first century, Yemen faces many social and economic problems.

As Yemen enters the twenty-first century, the country is moving further away from its traditions of tribal politics and the rule of imams. When the two Yemens united in 1990, the Republic of Yemen became the first country on the Arabian Peninsula to have a government run by officials elected from multiple political parties. Yemen also has laws that protect freedom of speech and the rights of the individual. Today Yemenis enjoy a level of democracy and individual freedom that few of their neighbors have.

Still, the government faces serious challenges that unification alone cannot solve. According to sociologist Mouna

H. Hashem, after unification, "Political slogans throughout the country echoed the importance of Yemen unity, one people, and the rights of all citizens to equal economic and social development. Many believed that unification would herald a new era of democracy and prosperity in Yemen. Instead, what followed was a series of external and internal political and economic crises that paralyzed the country."[59]

TOO MANY WORKERS

Some of these crises, such as the economic problems, were years in the making. Because Yemen has yet to develop domestic industries, the country has long depended on money earned by Yemenis working in other countries. In the 1970s, many Yemenis worked in the oil industry in Saudi Arabia or nearby states, but in the 1980s, oil prices fell and jobs disappeared. Between 1980 and 1989, money sent home by Yemenis working abroad dropped from US$1.6 billion to about $400 million (U.S.). At that point, the economy of Yemen was so bad that the country could hardly have survived without foreign aid, which it received from many countries.

Iraq was particularly important to Yemen's economy as a trading partner and source of aid. Then in 1990 Iraq invaded Kuwait, a small country on the Persian Gulf. Yemen opposed Iraq's invasion and demanded that Iraq withdraw from Kuwait, but Yemen also complained about the foreign troops entering Saudi Arabia in preparation for the war to force Iraq's withdrawal. In the UN Security Council, Yemen voted against the use of force to remove Iraq from Kuwait.

Yemen's vote angered many Western and Arab countries, which then stopped or reduced aid to Yemen. Saudi Arabia also evicted the Yemenis working there. Between eight hundred thousand and 1 million Yemenis returned home. By some estimates, as a result of its stance, Yemen lost $1.7 billion in foreign aid, trade, and the money workers sent home each year.

Meanwhile, refugees fleeing war in Somalia and other African countries poured into Yemen. Yemen could not provide jobs, housing, or health care to so many new residents. Although Yemen's economy was growing at the time, the few new jobs being created required skilled workers; most refugees and returning migrants, however, were illiterate and prepared only to do unskilled labor. Unemployment jumped from about 7 percent in early 1989 to 40 percent in 1995. Estimates suggest that 20 to 40 percent of men in Yemen are still unemployed.

NOT ENOUGH TO GO AROUND

At the same time that unemployment was rising, food shortages caused prices to double between 1990 and 1992. Angry citizens staged demonstrations, which sometimes turned violent. Thousands of jobless people were homeless or lived in government-run tent cities. Without a way to earn money honestly, more people turned to crime, so crime rates rose.

Even people with decent jobs struggled to survive. As anthropologist Paul Dresch noted, "To live a quietly middle-class life in Sanaa at the end of the [1990s] (to run a car, clothe the children decently and send them to school…) cost about $1,000 a month. The official salary of a minister was about $US 200 per month."[60] Day laborers and people living in remote villages generally earned less than $50 per month.

High prices and a shortage of jobs mean that many Yemenis live in poverty. According to the United States Agency for International Development (USAID), Yemen is one of the world's twenty-five poorest and least developed countries. The number of people living in poverty doubled between 1992 and 1998, and up to 60 percent of Yemenis now live in poverty. Wealth remains concentrated among a few families, often those of political leaders or important sheikhs. Dresch comments, "Ordinary Yemenis, with their fields and their little shops, simply do not have access to much of the national wealth."[61]

GOVERNMENT POVERTY

The Yemeni government had money problems as well. When the two Yemens united, North Yemen was poor, and South Yemen was even poorer. Both countries owed large amounts of money to foreign governments and organizations. The new Yemeni government inherited debt equal to twice what the entire country produced in a year. That debt

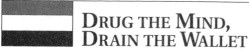

DRUG THE MIND, DRAIN THE WALLET

Almost all Yemeni men chew *qat*, and many women do as well. As a result, the production of this narcotic shrub is one of Yemen's biggest businesses. Estimates suggest that in the early 1990s *qat* production employed almost 20 percent of the workforce, used at least a quarter of the irrigated farmland, and earned the equivalent of 25 percent of the country's total value of goods and services.

Critics debate the damage *qat* does to the user's health. *Qat* is not physically addictive and has not been proven to have serious side effects. Some health problems are associated with *qat*, however, including insomnia, stomach pain, and liver and urinary problems for women.

The nation's economy may also be suffering from the production of *qat*. Farmers grow *qat* because the shrub can grow in poor soil, requires little water, and sells for a high price. While this is good for the individual farmer, so much land is dedicated to *qat* farming that Yemen is no longer producing enough food for its growing population. The country must import twice as much grain as it produces.

The use of *qat* may also cause financial hardship for a family. Many men spend more money on *qat* than on food for their families. A man may have

to spend an entire day's wages to buy enough *qat* for one *qat* chewing session; many men spend a quarter to half of their income on *qat*.

Yemenis continue to debate the value and risks of this drug. Scholar Tim Mackintosh-Smith writes in *Yemen: The Unknown Arabia* that "Yemenis themselves, while admitting that their habit is expensive, defend it on the grounds that it stimulates mental activity and concentration; they point out that at least the money spent on it remains within the national economy."

A Yemeni greedily chews qat.

A fruit dealer carries his load on a narrow road. Most Yemenis live in poverty.

increased during the civil war of 1994, and still Yemen's government spent more than it earned.

Yemen tried to solve this problem by simply printing more money. Instead of helping, however, this flood of new money led to high inflation. In the early 1990s, prices almost doubled some years. The government then tried to reduce its deficit by controlling spending. One way to reduce spending was to eliminate unnecessary government jobs. In 1997 Yemen had seven hundred thousand public employees, including the military—a huge number for a country that size. Many of these workers had little to do; in fact, one survey claimed that 40 percent of civil servants never even went to work. In order to reduce expenses, Yemen's leaders cut some thirty thousand government jobs.

In response to these measures, in 1997 Yemen's inflation rate finally dropped to around 10 percent each year. In the five years that followed, the inflation rate stayed between about 8 and 11 percent. Gradually, the government's income grew larger than its spending. An increase in worldwide oil prices helped bring in more money. In 2000 Yemen's government took in about $840 million more than it spent, thanks mainly to the sale of oil. In 2001, Yemen still owed over $4 billion, equal to about 80 percent of the country's yearly income. In order for Yemen to further reduce its debt, oil prices will have to remain high.

AID, OIL, AND INDUSTRY

To build a secure future, however, Yemen needs more than oil. The oil industry provides Yemen over $1 billion each year, nearly 70 percent of the government's income. However, oil prices can go up or down, and Yemen's oil exports are small compared with other Middle Eastern countries. Yemen produces less than half a percent of the world's oil output, and about a third of Yemen's oil stays within the country for local use. Oil alone is not enough to fund the government or to provide jobs for all workers.

In order to develop industry, Yemen needs resources such as water, energy, transportation, and skilled workers. Yemen has just a few exports, and steep, winding mountain roads make it difficult to transport goods within the country. Only 30 percent of the country has electricity, and public water is not always available even in large cities. In addition, high illiteracy and poor education mean that most people are untrained for anything but the most menial of jobs.

In 1995 Yemenis were once again allowed work visas in Saudi Arabia, though with more restrictions than in the past. Close to half a million Yemenis now work in Saudi Arabia, mostly as laborers or servants. At home in Yemen, workers may find jobs in one of the few factories, which produce cigarettes, soft drinks, processed foods, and products from plastic, rubber, and aluminum. The government is trying to create new jobs by expanding the port at Aden, with the hope that it will again become one of the world's busiest shipping ports. This would create jobs at the docks and in warehouses and would also bring in tax money.

Economic improvements will take time; meanwhile, Yemen depends on aid from the international community. Many countries renewed their aid to Yemen after the 1994 civil war, though they often sent less money than they had previously. Yemen now receives hundreds of millions of dollars in loans and grants from foreign countries and international organizations. This money helps Yemen develop its agriculture, roads, and health and educational systems. Yemen is trying to form closer bonds with other Arab and Western countries in the hopes of increasing foreign aid and trade.

CORRUPTION CUTS BUSINESS

Foreign aid helps in the short term, but it comes with the risk that the donors will someday stop their payments, as they did in 1990. For the long term, Yemen needs to build the domestic economy. Since few Yemenis have the money to start new businesses, the government is encouraging foreign companies to invest in Yemeni businesses.

However, corruption discourages many foreign firms from investing in Yemen despite great potential for trade. According to the U.S. Commercial Service, a unit of the U.S. Department of Commerce, "Bureaucratic corruption at all levels of government affects all aspects of doing business in Yemen."[62] When getting government permits and closing business deals, foreigners often find that good business plans are useless if one does not have a friend or relative in the government. Yemenis also expect gifts from people who want favors, and many Westerners interpret this old tradition as a demand for bribes.

In addition, embezzlement was common through the 1990s, and was rarely punished. Dresch cites one example in which "a man caught simply plundering the petrol company at home (on a massive scale) was not jailed or even forced to pay back his gains but appointed ambassador to a European capital."[63]

Putting an end to official corruption will be difficult. Because so many government employees are underpaid, the temptation to take bribes is strong. Family and tribal ties also persuade many people to offer special favors to their kin. To discourage corruption, Yemen will need to be able to pay government workers a living wage, but it will also need additional laws and stricter enforcement.

WASTED OPPORTUNITIES

To reduce its dependence on foreign aid, Yemen's government is hunting for other economic opportunities. For one thing, Yemen would like to develop its tourism industry. Indeed, Yemen has much to offer tourists: beautiful scenery, good weather, historic and archaeological sites, a coastline with sandy beaches, and scuba diving sites with coral reefs teeming with aquatic life. According to Michael Jenner, "Culture and climate are the two magnets which draw visitors. The country is ideally suited to small groups of interested individuals, keen to discover the unique archeological and architectural heritage of a forgotten corner of the world's civilisation."[64]

The government is trying to develop hotels, restaurants, and convention centers to lure more tourists. But Yemen's tourism industry suffers from the same lack of resources that limits other development efforts. The country has cheap accommodations for budget travelers but lacks midrange and luxury hotels. Bad roads and poor public transportation make it difficult to reach many of the sites that would appeal to tourists, such as the famous Marib Dam. The lack of safe drinking water, plumbing, and electricity in many areas might also discourage some travelers from visiting. In order for Yemen's tourism industry to expand, the country must improve these aspects of its infrastructure.

An even greater problem lies in the fact that some tourists have been kidnapped in Yemen. The tribes of Yemen are fiercely independent and well armed with automatic weapons. Since 1990 over one hundred kidnappings have taken place in Yemen. Many victims were businessmen and politicians in Sanaa, but a number of tourists were also snatched. According to Pertti Hamalainen,

A tribesman buys a grenade launcher from a dealer. Fearful of violence, many tourists avoid Yemen.

> A typical, nonviolent, kidnapping proceeds as follows: the kidnapped victim is transferred to a remote village. The kidnappers then present demands for their tribe. These can be for better infrastructure, for better channels to the centres of power, or even for a reversal of a judge's decision. While negotiations proceed hostages are treated well…. If the tribe feels safe, the hostages can walk around and socialise with the villagers, who are usually friendly towards their "guests."[65]

Very few of these kidnappings have resulted in the death of tourists, but the threat is still enough to discourage many would-be visitors.

For many years the Yemeni government gave in to kidnappers' demands and paid for the release of victims. Eventually, officials decided that this only encouraged more kidnappings, and so they changed their tactics. Since 1998 kidnappers have faced harsh penalties, including the death penalty for the group's leader. As a result, the kidnapping of foreigners has declined.

EVEN GREATER RISKS

The terrorist attack on the USS Cole *in 2000 had severe economic repercussions for Yemen.*

Yemen's government faces an even more serious challenge in its attempts to lure tourists and foreign businesses: Yemen has a reputation as a haven for Islamic terrorists who want to attack Western interests. Several high-profile incidents have given many Westerners the idea that Yemen is a dangerous enemy instead of an investment opportunity.

The American government, for one, has told its citizens not to travel to Yemen for any reason. The U.S. State Department warns, "The September 11 [2001] terrorist attacks in the United States elevated security concerns for Americans in Yemen that already were high, following a number of terrorist actions and kidnapping incidents over the past few years."[66] Warnings such as these discourage Americans from bringing their business or tourist dollars to Yemen.

Even before the September 11 attacks, terrorism was costing Yemen. In October 2000, al-Qaeda terrorists bombed the USS *Cole*, a navy ship in port at Aden, killing seventeen American sailors. That incident cost Yemen some $300 million in lost investments and tourism. The attack also gave Yemen a reputation for harboring terrorists, which discouraged many countries from sending their ships to Aden.

The Yemeni government has been working with the U.S. FBI to find and arrest terrorists. Karl Vick, writing for the *Washington Post* in September 2001, said, "Of all the Arab nations walking a tightrope since President Bush demanded that every country choose sides in the war on terrorism, perhaps none has stepped livelier than Yemen."[67]

Yet Vick noted the challenges Yemen faces in controlling terrorists: "Yemen has a thousand miles of unpatrolled coast, another thousand miles of wide-open frontier and a government that struggles to assert its authority beyond major towns."[68] Most Yemenis do not yet feel loyalty to their nation. Instead, they feel loyal to small groups, such as their village. Tribes function like small countries, with their own unwritten laws and courts for settling disputes. Many Yemenis do not trust the government, which has little influence in remote towns. Thus, newly trained antiterrorist police may not find terrorists hiding in secluded villages if local people fail to cooperate. In addition, ending Yemen's reputation for violence is a struggle in a country where men commonly carry automatic weapons.

According to political professor Stephen Zunes, "The presence of a large number of Al-Qaida members and sympathizers within the country is a reflection not of government support or complicity, but the general lawlessness of this impoverished society, where clan and tribe often carry more authority than the state."[69]

WOOING THE WEST

Yemen's ability to control terrorism is important to many countries, especially the United States. According to USAID,

> Yemen's economic and political development is essential for achieving the key U.S. goal of stability in the Gulf region…. Yemen is critical to U.S. counterterrorism interests in the post–September 11th environment, and the United States will work with the Government of Yemen to deal with terrorists on Yemeni soil and to deter terrorists from seeking refuge in or transiting through Yemen.[70]

The United States and many European countries also want to see Yemen's democratic government succeed. A peaceful democracy in Yemen, American policy planners hope, might influence other Middle Eastern countries to embrace democracy. Many Westerners believe that democracy will bring peace to the Middle East by improving the lives of ordinary people.

Yemen is trying to convince the world that it has a healthy democracy. At a 1999 conference in Sanaa, Yemen voiced its resolve to encourage women and minorities to play a greater political role in the nation. Then the prime minister pointed out that Yemen needed financial support to preserve democracy. Yemen's leaders are striving for democracy in part for idealistic reasons and in part to lure Western businesses and aid money.

CAUGHT BETWEEN TWO WORLDS

Yemen's politicians must strike a delicate balance between the wishes of outsiders and the desires of their own people. Most Western countries want Yemen to be more like them, with guaranteed religious freedom, equality between men and women, and a legal system that protects the rights of individuals. Many Yemeni citizens also want the freedoms and opportunities of a modern democracy. They feel that they can be good Muslims and also have a Western-style political and social system. Other Yemenis, however, blame modernization for the increases in poverty and unemployment since

A masked member of an antiterrorist unit brandishes his weapon. Yemen is taking steps to control terrorism within its borders.

unification. These people, known as Islamists, think that the country should strictly follow Islamic law, which they believe would close the gap between rich and poor.

Many Islamists try to emulate the Prophet Muhammad and his family as they lived in the seventh century. They protest modern trends such as women going to school and working outside the home. Dresch notes, "In the period 1990–4 Islamists had become notorious for opposing the right of women to act in politics, for example, and it was often female members of such groups who did so."[71] In 1999 Islamist groups complained about the staff and curriculum of

Sanaa University's Women's Studies Center. In response, the center was closed and gender studies eliminated from the school's curriculum.

Islamists generally contend that many Western habits, such as the wearing of revealing clothing, dancing, and drinking alcohol, are sinful and should not be allowed. One southern Yemeni said, "Before the '94 war we were Socialist, but since then the fundamentalists are very powerful. For those people everything is haram [forbidden]: music, dancing, aeroplanes, qat, alcohol, even trousers!"[72]

FREEDOM OF THE PRESS

Yemeni law protects the freedom of the press, though Yemen has more restrictions than most Western countries. For example, the media cannot criticize Islam or the president as a person, though they can criticize the president's actions. The four largest papers in Yemen are government controlled, but the country has hundreds of other newspapers and magazines. Many of these are published by political parties and express the parties' differing views.

Complaints against the news media must be tried in court, though the police and military still sometimes harass publishers. Papers that print negative articles about the government have been charged with slander and sometimes forced to stop publication. Security forces have arrested and threatened reporters and editors. In 1990 Dr. Abdulaziz al-Saqqaf founded the *Yemen Times*, a popular English-language newspaper known for its criticism of the government. In the following decade he was arrested once and harassed many times. In 1995, al-Saqqaf became the first Arab journalist to win the International Prize for Freedom of the Press, an award presented by the U.S. National Press Club.

Regardless of how much freedom the Yemeni press has, newspapers are limited in their ability to reach people, since many Yemenis are illiterate. Radio and television are other ways of sharing information. Yemen has two TV stations, which broadcast from 4 P.M. to midnight and on Friday mornings. People can watch news coverage, local cultural programs, sports, cartoons, and comedies or soap operas, which are often filmed in Egypt or Syria. The government controls local television and radio stations, but satellite dishes allow some people to receive foreign broadcasts. The mountains make it hard to get reception in many towns, however, so word of mouth is still an important way of spreading news.

Islamist groups are especially popular in poor areas, where Islamic charities provide economic aid. The largest Muslim political group, Islah, provides food to the poor during Muslim holidays and helps young people pay for marriage. This kind of direct generosity appeals to people far more than the government's taxes and budget cuts, and makes Islah a potent force at election time.

The rise of conservative Islam is not assured, however. In 1997 Islah lost seats in Parliament. By 2002 Islah held just 64 seats, compared with the 223 of the General People's Congress (GPC). And even many Islah members want a modern Yemen. The party backed Ali Abdallah Salih for president. Salih heads the GPC, a liberal party committed to reform. The government continues to promise that it will promote democracy, as well as reform the economy and fight against corruption.

Observers continue to hope that the government's efforts will pay off. According to scholar Antoine Lonnet, "Within the Arab World, Yemen is a shining example of a country that invests heavily and carefully in the enormous human and natural wealth it has inherited from its very long history."[73] With persistence and luck, Yemen will find a way to balance the new and the old, opportunity and tradition, the outside world's demands and the local people's needs. Then perhaps once again Yemen can claim the title "Happy Arabia."

FACTS ABOUT YEMEN

GEOGRAPHY

Country name: *conventional long form:* Republic of Yemen; *conventional short form:* Yemen; *local long form:* Al Jumhuriyah al Yamaniyah; *local short form:* Al Yaman

Capital: Sanaa

Total area: 203,850 square miles (527,970 square kilometers)

Bordering countries: Saudi Arabia, Oman

PEOPLE

Population: 18,078,035 (July 2001 est.)

Ethnic composition: Predominantly Arab, with some Africans, South Asians, and Europeans

Language: Arabic

Literacy: total population: 38% (1990 est.)

    male: 53%

    female: 26%

Life expectancy at birth: Total population: 60 years (2001 est.)

    male: 58 years

    female: 62 years

Religion: Predominantly Muslim, including Sunni and Shiite, with small numbers of Jews, Christians, and Hindus

GOVERNMENT

Government type: Republic

Head of government: Prime Minister Abd al-Qadir al-Ba Jamal (2002)

Chief of state: President Ali Abdallah Salih (2002)

Executive branch: The president is elected for a seven-year term by a vote of all citizens over eighteen. The vice president, prime minister, and deputy prime ministers are appointed by the president. A Council of Ministers is appointed by the president with the advice of the prime minister.

Legislative branch: A constitutional amendment in 2001 created a two-part legislature. The Shura Council has 111 members, who are appointed by the president. The Council of Representatives has 301 members, who are elected by popular vote to serve six-year terms.

ECONOMY

Currency: Yemeni rial (YER)

Exchange rate: Yemeni rials per U.S. dollar: 164.59 (October 2000)

Occupations: Most people work in agriculture and herding. Construction, industry, services, and commerce employ less than one-quarter of the labor force.

Agricultural products: grain, fruits, vegetables, *qat*, coffee, cotton, livestock (sheep, goats, cattle, camels), dairy products, poultry, and fish

Natural resources: oil, rock salt, marble, small deposits of minerals

Industries: oil production and refining, food processing, handicrafts, aluminum products, cement, cotton textiles, and leather goods

Export commodities: crude oil, coffee, dried and salted fish

Export partners: Thailand, 34%; China, 26%; South Korea, 14%; Japan, 3%; (1999); other, 23%

NOTES

INTRODUCTION: AT THE CENTER OF THE WORLD

1. Eric Hansen, *Motoring with Mohammed: Journeys to Yemen and the Red Sea*. Boston: Houghton Mifflin, 1991, p. 175.

CHAPTER 1: THE GREEN LAND OF ARABIA

2. Michael Jenner, *Yemen Rediscovered*. London: Longman, 1983, p. 26.

3. Joseph B.F. Osgood, *Notes of Travel or Recollections of Majunga, Zanzibar, Muscat, Aden, Mocha, and Other Eastern Ports*. 1854. Reprint: Freeport, NY: Books for Libraries Press, 1972, p. 121.

4. Osgood, *Notes of Travel*, p. 185.

5. Jenner, *Yemen Rediscovered*, p. 24.

6. Quoted in Jenner, *Yemen Rediscovered*, p. 25.

7. H.J. Dumont, ed., *Soqotra: Proceedings of the First International Symposium on Soqotra Island: Present and Future*. New York: United Nations Publications, 1998.

CHAPTER 2: OCCUPATIONS AND INDEPENDENCE

8. Ismail I. Nawwab, Peter C. Speers, and Paul F. Hoye, eds., *Aramco and Its World*. Washington, DC: Arabian American Oil Company, 1980, p. 33.

9. Jenner, *Yemen Rediscovered*, p. 30.

10. Quoted in Jenner, *Yemen Rediscovered*, pp. 31–32.

11. Quoted in Nawwab, Speers, and Hoye, *Aramco and Its World*, p. 33.

12. Quoted in Pertti Hamalainen, *Yemen*. Victoria, Australia: Lonely Planet, 1999, p. 15.

13. Robin Bidwell, *The Two Yemens*. Essex, England: Longman Group and Westview Press, 1983, p. 5.

14. Jenner, *Yemen Rediscovered*, p. 40.

15. Jenner, *Yemen Rediscovered*, p. 45.

16. Bidwell, *The Two Yemens*, p. xvi.

17. Bidwell, *The Two Yemens*, pp. 16–17.

18. Bidwell, *The Two Yemens*, p. 18.

19. Bidwell, *The Two Yemens*, p. 22.

20. Bidwell, *The Two Yemens*, p. 27.

21. Quoted in Bidwell, *The Two Yemens*, p. 37.

Chapter 3: North and South Fight and Unite

22. Paul Dresch, *A History of Modern Yemen.* Cambridge, England: Cambridge University Press, 2000, p. 51.

23. Quoted in Dresch, *A History of Modern Yemen*, p. 50.

24. Quoted in Dresch, *A History of Modern Yemen*, p. 53.

25. Bidwell, *The Two Yemens*, p. 121.

26. Hamalainen, *Yemen*, p. 21.

27. Helen Lackner, "The Rise of the National Liberation Front as a Political Organisation," in B.R. Pridham, ed., *Contemporary Yemen: Politics and Historical Background.* London and Sydney, Australia: Croom Helm, 1984, p. 50.

28. Joseph Kostiner, *Yemen: The Tortuous Quest for Unity, 1990–94.* London: Royal Institute of International Affairs, 1996, p. 9.

29. Kostiner, *Yemen*, p. 1.

30. Quoted in Kostiner, *Yemen*, p. 6.

31. Dresch, *A History of Modern Yemen*, p. 192.

Chapter 4: Daily Life in Yemen

32. Richard F. Nyrop, ed., *The Yemens: Country Studies.* Washington, DC: American University, 1986, p. 124.

33. Dresch, *A History of Modern Yemen*, p. 207.

34. Nyrop, *The Yemens*, p. 110.

35. Nyrop, *The Yemens*, p. 110.

36. Tim Mackintosh-Smith, *Yemen: The Unknown Arabia.* Woodstock, NY: Overlook Press, 2000, p. 18.

37. Hamalainen, *Yemen*, p. 183.

38. Pascal Maréchaux, *Arabia Felix*. Woodbury, NY: Barron's, 1980, n.p.

39. Nyrop, *The Yemens*, p. 125.

40. Hansen, *Motoring with Mohammed*, p. 166.

41. Nyrop, *The Yemens*, p. 125.

42. Hamalainen, *Yemen*, p. 43.

43. Jenner, *Yemen Rediscovered*, pp. 145–46.

44. Nyrop, *The Yemens*, p. 107.

45. Hansen, *Motoring with Mohammed*, p. 157.

CHAPTER 5: THE ARTS OF YEMEN

46. Nawwab, Speers, and Hoye, *Aramco and Its World*, p. 61.

47. Quoted in Dresch, *A History of Modern Yemen*, p. 95.

48. Quoted in Andrea Shen, "Poetry as Power," *Harvard University Gazette*, December 9, 1999. www.news.harvard.edu.

49. Quoted in Rachel Galvin, "Of Poets, Prophets, and Politics," *Humanities*, January/February 2002. www.neh.gov.

50. Quoted in Yahya Yusef Al-Hodeidi, "Iskander Thabet: A Monument in Modern Yemeni Music History," *Yemen Times*, September 1994. www.aiys.org/webdate/iska.html.

51. A.D. Bakewell, "Traditional Music in the Yemen," *Journal of the British-Yemeni Society*, 1995. www.al-bab.com/bys.

52. Quoted in Al-Hodeidi, "Iskander Thabet."

53. Hamalainen, *Yemen*, p. 41.

54. Nyrop, *The Yemens*, p. 122.

55. Maréchaux, *Arabia Felix*, n.p.

56. Maréchaux, *Arabia Felix*, n.p.

57. Karen Dabrowska, "Visions of Yemen: Differing Perspectives of a Uniquely Beautiful Country," *Yemen Times*, November 13–19, 2000. www.yementimes.com.

58. Quoted in Tawfeek Al-Shara'abi, "Picturesque Display by International Women's Association," *Yemen Times*, June

12–18, 2000. www.yementimes.com.

CHAPTER 6: MODERN CHALLENGES

59. Mouna H. Hashem, *Goals for Social Integration and Realities of Social Exclusion in the Republic of Yemen.* Geneva, Switzerland: International Labour Organization, 1996, p. 41.

60. Dresch, *A History of Modern Yemen,* p. 206.

61. Dresch, *A History of Modern Yemen,* p. 204.

62. U.S. Commercial Service, *Yemen Country Commercial Guide FY2002.* www.usatrade.gov/website/ccg.nsf.

63. Dresch, *A History of Modern Yemen,* p. 204.

64. Jenner, *Yemen Rediscovered,* p. 155.

65. Hamalainen, *Yemen,* p. 59.

66. U.S. Department of State, Bureau of Consular Affairs, "Consular Information Sheet: Yemen." http://travel.state.gov.

67. Karl Vick, "Yemen Walks Tightrope in Terrorism Stance," *Washington Post* Foreign Service, September 29, 2001, p. A20.

68. Vick, "Yemen Walks Tightrope in Terrorism Stance," p. A20.

69. Stephen Zunes, "Yemen, the United States, and Al-Qaida," *Global Affairs Commentary,* December 19, 2001. www.foreignpolicy-infocus.org.

70. United States Agency for International Development, "Yemen Briefing," 2003. www.usaid.gov.

71. Dresch, *A History of Modern Yemen,* p. 200.

72. Quoted in Kevin Rushby, *Eating the Flowers of Paradise: A Journey Through the Drug Fields of Ethiopia and Yemen.* New York: St. Martin's Press, 1999, p. 228.

73. Antoine Lonnet, "The Soqotri Language: Past Present and future," in Dumont, *Soqotra,* p. 297.

CHRONOLOGY

1000 B.C.
Five city-states on the edge of the Eastern Desert are at the center of ancient trade routes.

A.D. 50
The Himyarites control southwestern Arabia.

300s and 400s
Jewish and Christian missionaries enter Arabia and convert many tribes.

525
Ethiopia invades Yemen.

570–632
The Prophet Muhammad lives in northern Arabia and founds the Islamic religion.

575
The Himyarites defeat the Ethiopians with the help of Persia, which then takes control of southern Arabia.

600s
Islam spreads through the Arabian Peninsula.

1515
Egypt conquers the Tihama and the mountains around Sanaa.

1517–1585
The Ottoman Turks slowly take control of Yemen.

1607–1636
The Zaydi tribe leads a rebellion that ousts the Turks.

1636–1658
The Zaydis expand their empire by conquering other tribes.

1720–1740
Yemen sells most of the world's coffee.

1728
The sultan of Lahej declares himself an independent ruler of the Aden region, starting a division between northern and southern Yemen.

1839
The British take Aden, which remains a British crown colony until 1967.

1849–1871
The Ottoman Turks seize control of northern Yemen.

1904–1911
Yahya ibn Mohammed leads the Zaydis in attacks on the Turks, until they give him control over most of northern Yemen.

1918
The treaty that ends World War I forces the Turks to withdraw from Yemen.

1934
Yahya and Britain sign a treaty that retains the British-Turkish border between northern and southern Yemen that was established in 1905.

February 17, 1948
Rebels assassinate Imam Yahya; his son, Ahmad, takes over North Yemen.

1962
Imam Ahmad dies; the army overthrows his son, Badr, and founds the Yemen Arab Republic.

1962–1970
Civil war in North Yemen rages between Badr's royalists and the rebel republicans.

1966–1967
The rebel National Liberation Front takes over many regions in South Yemen.

1967
Britain withdraws from South Yemen; the National Liberation Front founds the People's Republic of South Yemen.

1978
Colonel Ali Abdallah Salih becomes president of North Yemen.

1988
North and South Yemen fight over a border region where
both sides are hunting for oil; they eventually agree to explore for oil and minerals under a joint effort and announce
plans for unity.

1989–1990
The Soviet Union withdraws its support from South Yemen.

May 22, 1990
North and South Yemen unite as the Republic of Yemen.

August 2, 1990
Iraq invades Kuwait; Yemen opposes Iraq's invasion but
votes against the use of force to remove Iraq; as a result,
Western and Persian Gulf Arab countries cancel or reduce
aid to Yemen, and Saudi Arabia evicts the Yemenis working
there.

April 27, 1993
Elections for Parliament are held.

May 1994
The Republic of Yemen explodes in civil war as the south
tries to secede from the union.

July 1994
North Yemen's military conquers the resistance; the Yemens
remain unified, but the constitution is changed to more
closely follow north Yemen's Islamic practices.

September 1999
Yemen holds its first presidential elections through direct
voting; President Salih is reelected.

October 12, 2000
Al-Qaeda terrorists bomb the USS *Cole*, a navy ship in port
at Aden; the attacks damage Yemen's reputation in the Western world.

September 11, 2001
Al-Qaeda terrorists attack the World Trade Center in New
York City; the United States pressures Yemen to control
terrorism.

SUGGESTIONS FOR FURTHER READING

BOOKS

Robin Bidwell, *The Two Yemens.* Essex, England: Longman Group and Westview Press, 1983. A history of Yemen through 1981, with lots of entertaining anecdotes.

John Dunn, *The Spread of Islam.* San Diego: Lucent Books, 1996. A detailed history of Islam.

Matthew S. Gordon, *Islam: Origins, Practices, Holy Texts, Sacred Persons, Sacred Places.* New York: Oxford University Press, 2002. A balanced introduction to Islam, with color photographs and illustrations.

Eric Hansen, *Motoring with Mohammed: Journeys to Yemen and the Red Sea.* Boston: Houghton Mifflin, 1991. This entertaining book tells of Hansen's experiences during trips to Yemen in 1978 and 1988.

Michael Jenner, *Yemen Rediscovered.* London: Longman, 1983. A loving look at the people and history of Yemen, with lots of pictures.

Pascal Maréchaux, *Arabia Felix.* Woodbury, NY: Barrow's, 1980. Large color photographs accompany a short travel diary of the author's visits to Yemen.

WEBSITES

Central Intelligence Agency World Factbook (www.odci. gov/cia/publications/factbook). Statistics on the geography, people, government, and economy of Yemen.

U.S. Department of State (www.state.gov). "Background Notes: Yemen" provides a condensed history of Yemen, plus statistics on the economy, politics, and foreign relations.

U.S. Energy Information Administration (www.eia.doe. gov). "Country Analysis Brief: Yemen" contains background information on Yemen, focusing on the economy and industry, and includes links to other U.S. government sites.

Yemen Gateway (www.al-bab.com/yemen). The Yemen Gateway has information and articles from many sources, plus links to Yemeni organizations.

Yemen Times (www.yementimes.com). Yemen's weekly English newspaper is online, with a searchable archive.

Yemen Tourism.com (www.yementourism.com). Yemen's tourism board offers travel information about various sites and has articles on Yemen.

WORKS CONSULTED

BOOKS

Paul Dresch, *A History of Modern Yemen.* Cambridge, England: Cambridge University Press, 2000. A detailed account of twentieth-century Yemeni politics.

H.J. Dumont, ed., *Soqotra: Proceedings of the First International Symposium on Soqotra Island: Present and Future.* New York: United Nations Publications, 1998. A collection of scholarly essays on Socotra's people and environment.

Pertti Hamalainen, *Yemen.* Victoria, Australia: Lonely Planet, 1999. A guidebook to Yemen, with information about history, arts, and culture.

Mouna H. Hashem, *Goals for Social Integration and Realities of Social Exclusion in the Republic of Yemen.* Geneva, Switzerland: International Labour Organization, 1996. An analysis of how some groups are excluded from political and economic life in Yemen.

Joseph Kostiner, *Yemen: The Tortuous Quest for Unity, 1990–94.* London: Royal Institute of International Affairs, 1996. An in-depth look at the politics of Yemen in the first years after unity.

Tim Mackintosh-Smith, *Yemen: The Unknown Arabia.* Woodstock, NY: Overlook Press, 2000. Reminiscences of the author's experiences in Yemen.

Ismail I. Nawwab, Peter C. Speers, and Paul F. Hoye, eds., *Aramco and Its World.* Washington, DC: Arabian American Oil Company, 1980. This book mainly focuses on Saudi Arabia but contains some information on Yemen, plus details of Islamic history, writing, and literature.

Richard F. Nyrop, ed., *The Yemens: Country Studies.* Washington, DC: American University, 1986. A thorough discussion of the history, geography, politics, and economy of Yemen through the mid-1980s.

Joseph B.F. Osgood, *Notes of Travel or Recollections of Majunga, Zanzibar, Muscat, Aden, Mocha, and Other Eastern Ports.* 1854. Reprint: Freeport, NY: Books for Libraries Press, 1972.

A nineteenth-century American traveler's diary of a trip to Yemen and other countries.

B.R. Pridham, ed., *Contemporary Yemen: Politics and Historical Background*. London and Sydney, Australia: Croom Helm, 1984. Essays by various experts on the history and politics of Yemen, from an international symposium on contemporary Yemen.

Kevin Rushby, *Eating the Flowers of Paradise: A Journey Through the Drug Fields of Ethiopia and Yemen*. New York: St. Martin's Press, 1999. Rushby describes his travels and his experiences with *qat*.

PERIODICAL

Karl Vick, "Yemen Walks Tightrope in Terrorism Stance," *Washington Post* Foreign Service, September 29, 2001.

INTERNET SOURCES

Yahya Yusef Al-Hodeidi, "Iskander Thabet: A Monument in Modern Yemeni Music History," Yemen Times, September 1994. www.aiys.org/webdate/iska.html.

Tawfeek Al-Shara'abi, "Picturesque Display by International Women's Association," *Yemen Times*, June 12–18, 2000. www.yementimes.com.

A.D. Bakewell, "Traditional Music in the Yemen," *Journal of the British-Yemeni Society*, 1995. www.al-bab.com/bys.

Karen Dabrowska, "Visions of Yemen: Differing Perspectives of a Uniquely Beautiful Country," *Yemen Times*, November 13–19, 2000. www.yementimes.com.

Rachel Galvin, "Of Poets, Prophets, and Politics," *Humanities*, January/February 2002. www.neh.gov.

Andrea Shen, "Poetry as Power," *Harvard University Gazette*, December 9, 1999. www.news.harvard.edu.

United States Agency for International Development, "Yemen Briefing," 2003. www.usaid.gov.

U.S. Commercial Service, *Yemen Country Commercial Guide FY2002*. www.usatrade.gov/website/ccg.nsf.

U.S. Department of State, Bureau of Consular Affairs, "Consular Information Sheet: Yemen." http://travel.state.gov.

Stephen Zunes, "Yemen, the United States, and Al-Qaida," *Global Affairs Commentary*, December 19, 2001. www.foreignpolicy-infocus.org.

INDEX

Picture Credits

About the Author

Chris Eboch is the author of *The Well of Sacrifice*, a middle-grade historical adventure set in ninth-century Guatemala. *Turkey* was her first nonfiction book for Lucent; her second is *Yemen*. Eboch has visited more than twenty-five countries to indulge her love of history and travel. She studied photography at Rhode Island School of Design and writing at Emerson College. Eboch lives in New Mexico.